九紫火星命

Nine Purple Life Star

Feng Shui Essentials: Xuan Kong Nine Life Star
NINE PURPLE LIFE STAR

Copyright © 2011 by Joey Yap
All rights reserved worldwide.
Second Edition January 2013

All intellectual property rights contained or in relation to this book belongs to Joey Yap.

No part of this book may be copied, used, subsumed, or exploited in fact, field of thought or general idea, by any other authors or persons, or be stored in a retrieval system, transmitted or reproduced in any way, including but not limited to digital copying and printing in any form whatsoever worldwide without the prior agreement and written permission of the author.

The author can be reached at:

Mastery Academy of Chinese Metaphysics Sdn. Bhd. (611143-A)
19-3, The Boulevard, Mid Valley City,
59200 Kuala Lumpur, Malaysia.
Tel   : +603-2284 8080
Fax   : +603-2284 1218
Website : www.masteryacademy.com

DISCLAIMER:

The author, Joey Yap and the publisher, JY Books Sdn Bhd, have made their best efforts to produce this high quality, informative and helpful book. They have verified the technical accuracy of the information and contents of this book. Any information pertaining to the events, occurrences, dates and other details relating to the person or persons, dead or alive, and to the companies have been verified to the best of their abilities based on information obtained or extracted from various websites, newspaper clippings and other public media. However, they make no representation or warranties of any kind with regard to the contents of this book and accept no liability of any kind for any losses or damages caused or alleged to be caused directly or indirectly from using the information contained herein.

Published by JY Books Sdn. Bhd. (659134-T)

Table of content :

1	**LIFE STAR REFERENCE TABLE**	7
2	**INTRODUCTION**	12
3	**YOUR XUAN KONG LIFE STAR**	23
	Basic Attributes	24
4	**YOUR FENG SHUI ESSENTIALS**	27
	Directions	29
	Taking the Direction using a Compass	33
	Favorable Directions	39
	Unfavorable Directions	49
	Bed Alignment Direction	58
	Best Floor	60
	Personal Grand Duke Direction	65
	Personal Clash Direction	71
	Flying Star Effects	76
5	**THE FIVE ELEMENT**	97

6	**CHARACTERISTICS OF STAR**	109
	The Good	111
	The Bad	117
7	**CAREER AND WEALTH**	123
	Characteristics at work	124
	Suitable Job Roles	128
	Career and Wealth Guide	132
8	**RELATIONSHIPS**	139
	Guide for Relationships	140
9	**HEALTH**	145
	Guide for Health	146
10	**COMPATIBILITY with OTHER LIFE STARS**	151

LIFE STAR REFERENCE TABLE

Year Pillar and Gua Number Reference Table for 1912 - 2055

Animal	Year of Birth			Gua Number for Male	Gua Number for Female	Year of Birth			Gua Number for Male	Gua Number for Female
Rat	1912	壬子 Ren Zi	Water Rat	7	8	1936	丙子 Bing Zi	Fire Rat	1	5
Ox	1913	癸丑 Gui Chou	Water Ox	6	9	1937	丁丑 Ding Chou	Fire Ox	9	6
Tiger	1914	甲寅 Jia Yin	Wood Tiger	5	1	1938	戊寅 Wu Yin	Earth Tiger	8	7
Rabbit	1915	乙卯 Yi Mao	Wood Rabbit	4	2	1939	己卯 Ji Mao	Earth Rabbit	7	8
Dragon	1916	丙辰 Bing Chen	Fire Dragon	3	3	1940	庚辰 Geng Chen	Metal Dragon	6	9
Snake	1917	丁巳 Ding Si	Fire Snake	2	4	1941	辛巳 Xin Si	Metal Snake	5	1
Horse	1918	戊午 Wu Wu	Earth Horse	1	5	1942	壬午 Ren Wu	Water Horse	4	2
Goat	1919	己未 Ji Wei	Earth Goat	9	6	1943	癸未 Gui Wei	Water Goat	3	3
Monkey	1920	庚申 Geng Shen	Metal Monkey	8	7	1944	甲申 Jia Shen	Wood Monkey	2	4
Rooster	1921	辛酉 Xin You	Metal Rooster	7	8	1945	乙酉 Yi You	Wood Rooster	1	5
Dog	1922	壬戌 Ren Xu	Water Dog	6	9	1946	丙戌 Bing Xu	Fire Dog	9	6
Pig	1923	癸亥 Gui Hai	Water Pig	5	1	1947	丁亥 Ding Hai	Fire Pig	8	7
Rat	1924	甲子 Jia Zi	Wood Rat	4	2	1948	戊子 Wu Zi	Earth Rat	7	8
Ox	1925	乙丑 Yi Chou	Wood Ox	3	3	1949	己丑 Ji Chou	Earth Ox	6	9
Tiger	1926	丙寅 Bing Yin	Fire Tiger	2	4	1950	庚寅 Geng Yin	Metal Tiger	5	1
Rabbit	1927	丁卯 Ding Mao	Fire Rabbit	1	5	1951	辛卯 Xin Mao	Metal Rabbit	4	2
Dragon	1928	戊辰 Wu Chen	Earth Dragon	9	6	1952	壬辰 Ren Chen	Water Dragon	3	3
Snake	1929	己巳 Ji Si	Earth Snake	8	7	1953	癸巳 Gui Si	Water Snake	2	4
Horse	1930	庚午 Geng Wu	Metal Horse	7	8	1954	甲午 Jia Wu	Wood Horse	1	5
Goat	1931	辛未 Xin Wei	Metal Goat	6	9	1955	乙未 Yi Wei	Wood Goat	9	6
Monkey	1932	壬申 Ren Shen	Water Monkey	5	1	1956	丙申 Bing Shen	Fire Monkey	8	7
Rooster	1933	癸酉 Gui You	Water Rooster	4	2	1957	丁酉 Ding You	Fire Rooster	7	8
Dog	1934	甲戌 Jia Xu	Wood Dog	3	3	1958	戊戌 Wu Xu	Earth Dog	6	9
Pig	1935	乙亥 Yi Hai	Wood Pig	2	4	1959	己亥 Ji Hai	Earth Pig	5	1

- Please note that the date for the Chinese Solar Year starts on Feb 4. This means that if you were born in Feb 2 of 2002, you belong to the previous year 2001.

Xuan Kong Nine Life Star

Year Pillar and Gua Number Reference Table for 1912 - 2055

Animal	Year of Birth			Gua Number for Male	Gua Number for Female	Year of Birth			Gua Number for Male	Gua Number for Female
Rat	1960	庚子 Geng Zi	Metal Rat	4	2	1984	甲子 Jia Zi	Wood Rat	7	8
Ox	1961	辛丑 Xin Chou	Metal Ox	3	3	1985	乙丑 Yi Chou	Wood Ox	6	9
Tiger	1962	壬寅 Ren Yin	Water Tiger	2	4	1986	丙寅 Bing Yin	Fire Tiger	5	1
Rabbit	1963	癸卯 Gui Mao	Water Rabbit	1	5	1987	丁卯 Ding Mao	Fire Rabbit	4	2
Dragon	1964	甲辰 Jia Chen	Wood Dragon	9	6	1988	戊辰 Wu Chen	Earth Dragon	3	3
Snake	1965	乙巳 Yi Si	Wood Snake	8	7	1989	己巳 Ji Si	Earth Snake	2	4
Horse	1966	丙午 Bing Wu	Fire Horse	7	8	1990	庚午 Geng Wu	Metal Horse	1	5
Goat	1967	丁未 Ding Wei	Fire Goat	6	9	1991	辛未 Xin Wei	Metal Goat	9	6
Monkey	1968	戊申 Wu Shen	Earth Monkey	5	1	1992	壬申 Ren Shen	Water Monkey	8	7
Rooster	1969	己酉 Ji You	Earth Rooster	4	2	1993	癸酉 Gui You	Water Rooster	7	8
Dog	1970	庚戌 Geng Xu	Metal Dog	3	3	1994	甲戌 Jia Xu	Wood Dog	6	9
Pig	1971	辛亥 Xin Hai	Metal Pig	2	4	1995	乙亥 Yi Hai	Wood Pig	5	1
Rat	1972	壬子 Ren Zi	Water Rat	1	5	1996	丙子 Bing Zi	Fire Rat	4	2
Ox	1973	癸丑 Gui Chou	Water Ox	9	6	1997	丁丑 Ding Chou	Fire Ox	3	3
Tiger	1974	甲寅 Jia Yin	Wood Tiger	8	7	1998	戊寅 Wu Yin	Earth Tiger	2	4
Rabbit	1975	乙卯 Yi Mao	Wood Rabbit	7	8	1999	己卯 Ji Mao	Earth Rabbit	1	5
Dragon	1976	丙辰 Bing Chen	Fire Dragon	6	9	2000	庚辰 Geng Chen	Metal Dragon	9	6
Snake	1977	丁巳 Ding Si	Fire Snake	5	1	2001	辛巳 Xin Si	Metal Snake	8	7
Horse	1978	戊午 Wu Wu	Earth Horse	4	2	2002	壬午 Ren Wu	Water Horse	7	8
Goat	1979	己未 Ji Wei	Earth Goat	3	3	2003	癸未 Gui Wei	Water Goat	6	9
Monkey	1980	庚申 Geng Shen	Metal Monkey	2	4	2004	甲申 Jia Shen	Wood Monkey	5	1
Rooster	1981	辛酉 Xin You	Metal Rooster	1	5	2005	乙酉 Yi You	Wood Rooster	4	2
Dog	1982	壬戌 Ren Xu	Water Dog	9	6	2006	丙戌 Bing Xu	Fire Dog	3	3
Pig	1983	癸亥 Gui Hai	Water Pig	8	7	2007	丁亥 Ding Hai	Fire Pig	2	4

- Please note that the date for the Chinese Solar Year starts on Feb 4. This means that if you were born in Feb 2 of 2002, you belong to the previous year 2001.

Year Pillar and Gua Number Reference Table for 1912 - 2055

Animal	Year of Birth			Gua Number for Male	Gua Number for Female	Year of Birth			Gua Number for Male	Gua Number for Female
Rat	2008	戊子 Wu Zi	Earth Rat	1	5	2032	壬子 Ren Zi	Water Rat	4	2
Ox	2009	己丑 Ji Chou	Earth Ox	9	6	2033	癸丑 Gui Chou	Water Ox	3	3
Tiger	2010	庚寅 Geng Yin	Metal Tiger	8	7	2034	甲寅 Jia Yin	Wood Tiger	2	4
Rabbit	2011	辛卯 Xin Mao	Metal Rabbit	7	8	2035	乙卯 Yi Mao	Wood Rabbit	1	5
Dragon	2012	壬辰 Ren Chen	Water Dragon	6	9	2036	丙辰 Bing Chen	Fire Dragon	9	6
Snake	2013	癸巳 Gui Si	Water Snake	5	1	2037	丁巳 Ding Si	Fire Snake	8	7
Horse	2014	甲午 Jia Wu	Wood Horse	4	2	2038	戊午 Wu Wu	Earth Horse	7	8
Goat	2015	乙未 Yi Wei	Wood Goat	3	3	2039	己未 Ji Wei	Earth Goat	6	9
Monkey	2016	丙申 Bing Shen	Fire Monkey	2	4	2040	庚申 Geng Shen	Metal Monkey	5	1
Rooster	2017	丁酉 Ding You	Fire Rooster	1	5	2041	辛酉 Xin You	Metal Rooster	4	2
Dog	2018	戊戌 Wu Xu	Earth Dog	9	6	2042	壬戌 Ren Xu	Water Dog	3	3
Pig	2019	己亥 Ji Hai	Earth Pig	8	7	2043	癸亥 Gui Hai	Water Pig	2	4
Rat	2020	庚子 Geng Zi	Metal Rat	7	8	2044	甲子 Jia Zi	Wood Rat	1	5
Ox	2021	辛丑 Xin Chou	Metal Ox	6	9	2045	乙丑 Yi Chou	Wood Ox	9	6
Tiger	2022	壬寅 Ren Yin	Water Tiger	5	1	2046	丙寅 Bing Yin	Fire Tiger	8	7
Rabbit	2023	癸卯 Gui Mao	Water Rabbit	4	2	2047	丁卯 Ding Mao	Fire Rabbit	7	8
Dragon	2024	甲辰 Jia Chen	Wood Dragon	3	3	2048	戊辰 Wu Chen	Earth Dragon	6	9
Snake	2025	乙巳 Yi Si	Wood Snake	2	4	2049	己巳 Ji Si	Earth Snake	5	1
Horse	2026	丙午 Bing Wu	Fire Horse	1	5	2050	庚午 Geng Wu	Metal Horse	4	2
Goat	2027	丁未 Ding Wei	Fire Goat	9	6	2051	辛未 Xin Wei	Metal Goat	3	3
Monkey	2028	戊申 Wu Shen	Earth Monkey	8	7	2052	壬申 Ren Shen	Water Monkey	2	4
Rooster	2029	己酉 Ji You	Earth Rooster	7	8	2053	癸酉 Gui You	Water Rooster	1	5
Dog	2030	庚戌 Geng Xu	Metal Dog	6	9	2054	甲戌 Jia Xu	Wood Dog	9	6
Pig	2031	辛亥 Xin Hai	Metal Pig	5	1	2055	乙亥 Yi Hai	Wood Pig	8	7

- Please note that the date for the Chinese Solar Year starts on Feb 4. This means that if you were born in Feb 2 of 2002, you belong to the previous year 2001.

To download your Nine Purple Life Star Reference Chart FREE go to

www.masteryacademy.com/regbook

Here is your unique code for access:

GBSN6019

Your Life Star

Everyone falls under the jurisdiction of one of the 9 Life Stars and this will have different consequences for everyone. Your Life Star describes your key skills, characteristics and traits. Some people are creative but reserved, some people are aggressive and driven. What self destructive traits do you have? Do you have a bloated sense of pride or are you prone to gossip? Your Life Star can shine some light on the complexity of your personality and your good and bad traits.

Study of the Life Stars has practical benefits for everyone; it gives you valuable information about others in addition to yourself. Different Life Stars bestow different abilities on people which means that people belonging to each Star will exhibit different characteristics at work. A Star 1 person is diplomatic so they are best suited to roles demanding diplomacy, for example. Accordingly, employers can study the Xuan Kong Life Stars when making work place decisions whilst employees can use the system to help them go about working productively with their colleagues and superiors, even when disagreements arise.

If you become aware of your own harmful tendencies then you can learn to minimize them so you can advance. Similar benefits can be seen in romantic relationships and friendships. Learning that a Star 7 individual needs their space and independence

might help you accommodate this in your dealings with them when you might otherwise have been tempted to be clingy and dependant.

When we understand more about ourselves we can stop ourselves from making mistakes and perhaps forgive certain behaviour in others once we understand where it comes from.

Compatibility Guide

Certain people are, of course, more compatible with each other than others. In partnerships or relationships this takes on a new level of importance. Different Life Stars bestow the qualities of different elements on different people; for example, a Star 1 person has the qualities of water whilst a Star 7 person has the qualities of the Yin Metal element. Just as the elements control, pacify and weaken one another, individuals of the different Stars may dominate, clash with or enrich one another. This book includes a write up of how compatible different Stars are with one another. You may find that a relationship as a Star 1 person with a Star 5 person simply isn't worth the effort. A compatibility guide on each interaction gives you tips on how to best deal with the other Stars for mutual benefit, even taking into account your differences.

Compatible With BaZi Profiling Systems

If you are familiar with the **BaZi Profiling System** then you will be aware that, at first glance, it seems to deal with very similar issues. It can tell us about other preferences and internal view of the world. Do we have an optimistic view of things? Do we blame ourselves too much?

While there is some overlap between the jurisdiction of the Xuan Kong Life Star system and BaZi Profiling System, they are two different systems. They both deal with individual people and their personalities but they are not mutually exclusive. In fact, when studied together, they can be thought of as two pieces of the same puzzle.

The BaZi Profiling System tells us about ourselves and about others. It even tells us things that cannot be observed about others (things people do not communicate). What it can't tell us is how the outside environment plays into the picture. The Xuan Kong Nine Stars help determine *which* qualities are brought out and by what features and external forms in the environment.

Once we know what directions are conducive to good Qi, how external forms (pylons etc) can compound problems related to sectors in the home, which areas of our environment increase the risk of which ailments or even which people can create problems in our lives (compatibility guide) then we can begin shaping our external environment to whatever degree necessary in order to enjoy the most happiness, wealth and success. Xuan Kong Feng Shui

tells you precisely what effect the environment and compass directions will have on which people.

If you are simply interested in learning what makes a person tick rather than making decisions about an ideal environment for them to thrive in then I recommend you take up further study of the BaZi Profiling System. The goal of BaZi is to pinpoint personal deficiencies so that they may be overcome or to highlight personal strengths so that they may be capitalised on.

If you are trying to configure your environment in order to maximize the benefits that your home or place of work bestow upon you in terms of health, wealth and relationships, then the Feng Shui Xuan Kong Life Star system is the one for you.

When you combine the two systems and employ them on yourself you will be able to make the most of your best qualities and then seek out an environment which lets you shine and gives the least resistance. A powerful combination of self improvement and informed decision making!

An Easier Life

Life doesn't have to be difficult. It is possible to effectively dodge conflict, problem situations and health problems if you know they are coming. The Life Stars hold the key to many of the "surprises" that life has in store for us and we can learn to shape our environment to our own advantage. This is exciting stuff! Seeking out the best romantic relationships and business opportunities is a top priority for most people and the power of your Life Star can be called upon in these pursuits.

Even though much is made of the layout of the home with relation to Feng Shui, you won't need to bend over backwards to accommodate the advice given in this book. For instance, where you cannot choose the ideal living floor specified, second and third choices are mentioned. You can take as much or as little from this book as you need without fear of it making you paranoid and prey to "paralysis by analysis". Looking back on your own life, you can most probably think of two or three big mistakes – a bad business deal or choice in romantic partner, perhaps. Avoiding pitfalls of this magnitude in the future is made a whole lot easier when you have some idea of how likely they are to occur. If you can make changes to your environment to further reduce this likelihood then all the better!

I hope that this book expands your world view. Once you know how to utilize them, the Nine Stars can be the harbinger of great fortune instead of misery for you. If you can stay on the 'correct side' of your Star and always position yourself to bask in its positive influence then many happy successes await you.

Joey Yap
July, 2011

 www.facebook.com/joeyyapFB

Author's personal website :
www.joeyyap.com

Academy websites :
www.masteryacademy.com | www.maelearning.com |
www.baziprofiling.com

九紫火星命

Nine Purple Life Star

Life Star 9	Born in
Male	1928, 1937, 1946, 1955, 1964 1973, 1982, 1991, 2000, 2009
Female	1922, 1931, 1940, 1949. 1958 1967, 1976, 1985, 1994, 2003

- Please note that the date for the Chinese Solar Year starts on Feb 4. This means that if you were born in Feb 2 of 2002, you belong to the previous year 2001.

Your Xuan Kong Life Star

Your Xuan Kong Life Star is Gua #9, and your trigram is called Li. It looks like this:

For the rest of this book, we will refer to your Gua #9 as Life Star 9.

Basic Attributes of Star 9

Your Life Star 9 is of the Fire element, and as such, shares some of the traits associated with Fire. Fire in this case can refer to the flame of a small candle or the warmth of the sun. Being endowed with the qualities of the sun, you represent the season of summer. The colors red, pink and purple are associated with the Fire element.

As a Life Star 9, you possess the characteristics of warmth, generosity, and enthusiasm. You love to shine like the sun and to be appreciated. Like fire, you burn tirelessly in order to bring warmth and light into the lives of others, as well. You can be nurturing and selfless when it comes to supporting other people and motivating them to do things. As such, others tend to like you once they get to know you.

It is fair to say, however, that like a flickering flame on a candle you can also be incredibly mercurial and even fickle-minded. Furthermore, you have a tendency to depend on others to get things done and lack the ability to cultivate self-reliance. You can also be a perfectionist, which leaves you mulling over small details to the detriment of the larger picture. This means you may have a hard time completing things once you start them!

Basic Emotions & Temperament

Plus : Calm, foresightful, intelligent, generous, charismatic

Minus: Impulsive, fickle, inconsiderate, repetitive

YOUR FENG SHUI ESSENTIALS

The Feng Shui Essentials comprise Feng Shui Directions, the effects of the Xuan Kong Nine Stars in various sectors and areas of your home and workspace, and the Five Elements.

Each of these factors interact with your Life Star in different ways that will affect how your Life Star manifests itself and determine whether or not it brings out good or bad qualities in you.

方向

Directions

Directions

Direction is an integral component of understanding Xuan Kong Nine Life Stars. Different directions in your home and your place of work can either accentuate or depreciate the strength of your Life Star.

Favorable Direction will highlight or enhance the positive traits of your Life Star, while an Unfavorable Direction will diminish or weaken your Life Star and bring out some of its negative attributes.

The Life Star numbers are categorized into two groups: the East Group and the West Group. The names 'East Group' and 'West Group' are just to demarcate the Greater and Lesser Yin transformation of the Tai Ji. They do not literally represent directions.

East Group Life Stars include 1, 3, 4 and 9. Those who are Life Stars 2, 6, 7 and 8 belong to the West Group. The following table will give you a quick reference of the Auspicious and Inauspicious compass directions of the East and West Group.

East Group 東命

卦 Gua	生氣 Shen Qi Life Generating	天醫 Tian Yi Heavenly Doctor	延年 Yan Nian Longevity	伏位 Fu Wei Stability	禍害 Huo Hai Mishaps	五鬼 Wu Gui Five Ghosts	六煞 Liu Sha Six Killings	絕命 Jue Ming Life Threatening
坎 Kan 1 Water	東南 South East	東 East	南 South	北 North	西 West	東北 North East	西北 North West	西南 South West
震 Zhen 3 Wood	南 South	北 North	東南 South East	東 East	西南 South West	西北 North West	東北 North East	西 West
巽 Xun 4 Wood	北 North	南 South	東 East	東南 South East	西北 North West	西南 South West	西 West	東北 North East
離 Li 9 Fire	東 East	東南 South East	北 North	南 South	東北 North East	西 West	西南 South West	西北 North West

West Group 西命

卦 Gua	生氣 Shen Qi Life Generating	天醫 Tian Yi Heavenly Doctor	延年 Yan Nian Longevity	伏位 Fu Wei Stability	禍害 Huo Hai Mishaps	五鬼 Wu Gui Five Ghosts	六煞 Liu Sha Six Killings	絕命 Jue Ming Life Threatening
坤 Kun 2 Earth	東北 North East	西 West	西北 North West	西南 South West	東 East	東南 South East	南 South	北 North
乾 Qian 6 Metal	西 West	東北 North East	西南 South West	西北 North West	東南 South East	東 East	北 North	南 South
兌 Dui 7 Metal	西北 North West	西南 South West	東北 North East	西 West	北 North	南 South	東南 South East	東 East
艮 Gen 8 Earth	西南 South West	西北 North West	西 West	東北 North East	南 South	北 North	東 East	東南 South East

The concepts of Favorable and Unfavorable are derived from the Eight Wandering Stars system of the Ba Zhai Eight Mansion Feng Shui 八宅風水.

Each of the 8 directions is governed by a Star. These Wandering Stars will affect each Xuan Kong Life Star in different ways. Each Life Star has four Favorable Directions governed by Auspicious Stars: Sheng Qi 生氣 (Life Generating), Tian Yi 天醫 (Heavenly Doctor), Yan Nian 延年 (Longevity), and Fu Wei 伏位 (Stability).

The four Unfavorable Directions are governed by Inauspicious Stars and include Huo Hai 禍害 (Mishaps), Wu Gui 五鬼 (Five Ghost), Liu Sha 六煞 (Six Killings) and Jue Ming 絕命 (Life Diminishing).

The following diagram shows you the Favorable and Unfavorable Directions for Star 9.

Taking the Direction using a Compass

You will need a compass – or alternatively, the Joey Yap iLuoPan app for iPhone available at the Apple App Store – to determine the direction of your Main Door, Bed and Stove. Hold your compass or iLuoPan at waist level as shown on the illustration below. Your compass or iLuoPan will align to the magnetic North on its own. All you need to know is how to take your direction as indicated on the following pages.

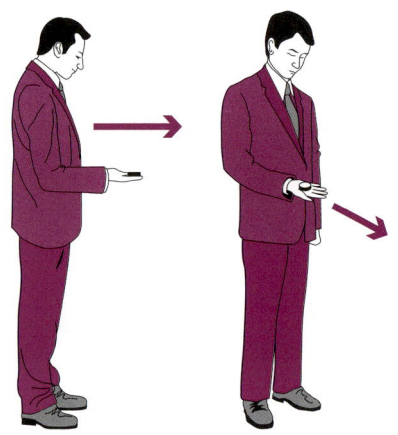

Facing Direction of the Main Door

1. Stand about one foot outside the door looking outwards.

2. Use the square base of your compass to help you align yourself parallel to the door.

3. Read the facing direction on your compass.

Facing Direction of the Bed

1. Measure from the head of the bed where your head is placed when you lie down (the direction the headboard faces) and not the direction your feet face.

Facing Direction of the Stove

1. For modern (gas or electric) stoves, look at the where direction of the cooking knobs (fire igniters) are pointing to determine its facing direction.

2. For traditional stoves that require wood and fire to work, look for their 'fire mouth' as the facing direction.

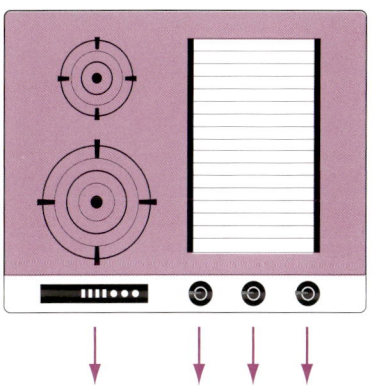

Favorable Directions

East

東 (82.6°-97.5°)

Life Generating
生氣 *(Sheng Qi)*

 The basic characteristics of the Sheng Qi Star:

It brings about promotions, career advancements, strong money and wealth luck, potential political power and authority, and all-round success.

The Sheng Qi Star represents life-generating Qi or energy. It also represents the Wood Element, and hence, governs the facets of success, authority, nobility, status and wealth in life. Wood relates to growth and advancement in life, and as such is an extremely auspicious Star to tap into. For you, the East direction taps into the Sheng Qi potential.

This Star is suitable for business (commercial), career and wealth-related pursuits. It would therefore be ideal for a business or residence to have its Main Door situated in the Sheng Qi sector as it allows you to tap into these energies to create opportunities for profit and long term wealth opportunities.

Sheng Qi is an active star by nature and thus, it is not conducive for rest or sleep-related activities. It is best to avoid having the bed or bedroom located in this sector or for anyone to sleep facing this direction. Use this sector for your work or for active pursuits instead of relaxing ones.

If this sector is missing from a house or is lacking in the office or the premises of a business, the wealth-related aspects of your career or venture will be considerably weakened and it will be a difficult struggle to amass wealth and prosperity.

Southeast
東南 (127.6°-142.5°)

Heavenly Doctor
天醫 (Tian Yi)

The basic characteristics of the Tian Yi Star:

It brings about general good luck and well-being, as well as positive mentor luck or the presence of sound advisors and guidance.

This Star represents the Earth Element and is therefore the determinant of noble people (mentors) and people of caliber and status. It also denotes your health prospects and physical wellbeing. As such, the Tian Yi Star is best utilized to help generate guidance for your career or for any project which you've embarked upon. It will bring about the help and assistance of others.

It is also a useful Star for health purposes, and its benefits can be employed when you need to recuperate, recover, or heal from an illness, surgical procedure or health issue.

When the Tian Yin sector is missing from a home or office, your health is likely to suffer because of it. In addition, you will also find help from noble people hard to come by, especially in times of need in life and career matters. You will come across more obstacles and obstructions which you must overcome on your own without the external help of others.

Since the Tian Yi Star represents nobility, it also governs your reputation, respectability, and your oratory powers. It thus has influence on your powers of speech and persuasion, and has some bearing on how you are perceived by others and how well they respond to your verbal overtures.

North
北 (352.6°-7.5°)

Longevity
延年 *(Yan Nian)*

The basic characteristics of the Yan Nian Star:

It prolongs and enhances life and improves the quality of your life. It promotes good communication with others which in turn makes for good relationships.

The Yan Nian Star represents the Metal Element, and as such governs speech and the effectiveness of your words. If you are looking to establish good relationships and rapport with others, you will need the help of this Star, since it governs aspects of successful networking, communication and relationship building.

The Yan Nian Star is important for family harmony and domestic bliss. It is also necessary if you wish to build good relationships with co-workers and colleagues. Essentially, it paves the way for smooth interpersonal relations, seldom plagued by misunderstanding, arguments and flare-ups. As such, the presence of the Yan Nian Star is useful for maintaining harmony.

If you are employed in public relations or marketing and you must interact with clients and customers as part of your daily routine, you will find the Qi brought about by this Star very useful to your career.

Do note that if the Yan Nian sector is missing, harmony and unity will be adversely affected, and relations are likely to be tense or strained. At the very least, you can expect more argument and discord with others.

South
南 (172.6°-187.5°)

Stability
伏位 (Fu Wei)

The basic characteristics of the Fu Wei Star:

It is a Star that promotes calm and keeps you grounded. It allows for peace of mind and rationality. It also promotes good luck.

The Fu Wei Star represents the Wood Element. When qualities or virtues such as calmness and tranquility are required, this is the Star you need! It promotes peace of mind and heightens clarity of thought, so this is also the Star to use if you need to focus, study or make important decisions.

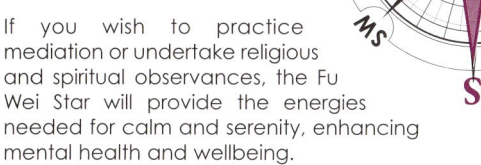

If you wish to practice mediation or undertake religious and spiritual observances, the Fu Wei Star will provide the energies needed for calm and serenity, enhancing mental health and wellbeing.

This Star is most suitably applied to libraries, study areas/zones or other places where concentration is necessary. When considering the home or workplace, this Star can help create areas where the mind can be easily quietened and people can reflect and turn inward.

When the Fu Wei sector is missing from a place, peace of mind will be difficult to attain.

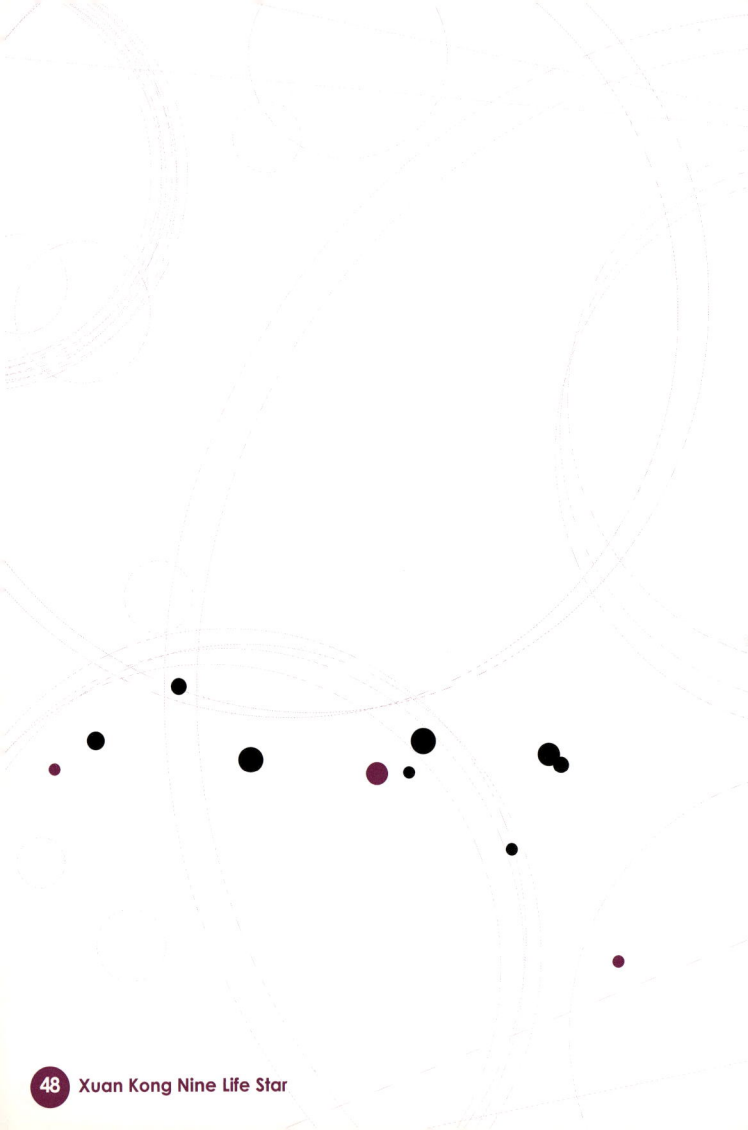

Unfavorable Directions

Northeast
東北 (37.6°-52.5°)

Mishaps
禍害 (Huo Hai)

The basic characteristics of the Huo Hai Star: It denotes potential calamities, accidents, and mishaps. It undermines good efforts and brings about the risk of mistakes and errors.

The Huo Hai Star represents the Earth Element and is the harbinger of mishaps, loss of wealth, sudden (unfortunate) changes or hassles as well as work-related obstacles. What it does is undermine your efforts and bring about sudden obstructions or problems that will result in a loss of time and energy.

If, for example, the Main Door of a property is located in this direction, you can reasonably expect to encounter quite a few obstacles and problems in your daily life. It is best to work around this area particularly if your main door or office is located in the West sector.

The detrimental effects of a negative star are compounded when it is located within an area that is already affected by negative Feng Shui, so pay attention to the negative structures outside this area.

West
西 (262.6°-277.5°)

Five Ghosts
五鬼 (Wu Gui)

The basic characteristics of the Wu Gui Star:

It brings about betrayal and treachery through back-stabbing, gossip, and rumors. It also denotes endless bickering and fraught tension brought about by arguments.

The Wu Gui Star represents the Fire Element and is the bringer of betrayal, ill-intentioned gossip, rumours, backstabbing, cruelty, petty people and even subterfuge and sabotage. It generally denotes a sense of unease brought upon by less-than-honest speech.

The presence of Wu Gui in a house causes disloyalty and discord amongst family members, affecting relationships and marriages. If it is present in your work place, then you should also watch out for fights and arguments between your colleagues or subordinates and friction or tension with your superiors.

Negative external forms such as (sharp) pylons and jagged rooftops pointing towards a house further aggravate the effects of this Star.

Southwest
西南 (217.6°-232.5°)

Six Killings
六煞 (Liu Sha)

The basic characteristics of the Liu Sha Star:

This Star brings about injuries and accidents. It also denotes the possibility of betrayals and dishonesty, and the risk of potential scandals.

The Liu Sha Star relates to the element of Water and is the harbinger of lawsuits and potential scandals. Legal problems at the workplace or adulterous affairs in relation to your marriage or personal relationships could be brought to light.

This Star is also the harbinger of bodily injury, harm and conditions requiring people to undergo physical surgery. Robberies and theft are also likely, and you will have to be careful about what information you share with others and with the general safety of your personal documents and possessions.

Be mindful of the presence of negative external forms, which will compound the adverse effects of this Star. For instance, a Y-shaped road at the Liu Sha sector will result in scandalous affairs, while negative structures as mentioned earlier will compound and exacerbate the harmful effects of the Liu Sha Star.

Northwest
西北 (307.6°-322.5°)

Life Threatening
絕命 (Jue Ming)

The basic characteristics of the Jue Ming Star:

It brings about the risk of accidents and major illness, and the threat of miscarriage for pregnant women. It also signals potential for great calamity.

This Star represents the Metal Element and it signifies accidents and illnesses. The energies of the Jue Ming Star are quite severe and so are its adverse effects, bringing with it considerable risk.

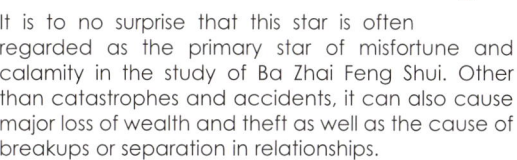

In severe cases, the Jue Ming Star can even cause fatal accidents, ailments or injuries when there are negative external forms outside of the Northwest sector.

It is to no surprise that this star is often regarded as the primary star of misfortune and calamity in the study of Ba Zhai Feng Shui. Other than catastrophes and accidents, it can also cause major loss of wealth and theft as well as the cause of breakups or separation in relationships.

Bed Alignment Direction

One of the key Feng Shui factors of the bedroom is how your bed is placed. For starters, your bed should preferably be pushed against a wall, with the headboard also against it. The most important thing you can do when laying out your bedroom with regards to Feng Shui is to make sure your headboard is aligned with your Favorable Direction.

Facing Direction, in the case of bed alignment, refers to the direction of your headboard. This means it is the direction your head faces when you lie down on the bed, and **not** the direction that your feet face.

As a Star 9, your Bed Alignment Directions are:

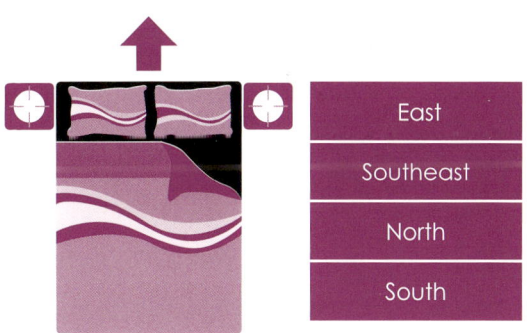

East

Southeast

North

South

Best Floor

A reality of modern life is that most of us do not live in houses these days, instead living in multi story apartments and condominium blocks.

Some of us are pretty mobile and live a nomad-like lifestyle that may require us to stay in high-rise buildings for certain periods of time. As such, it becomes important to select the right floor to reside in. The objective of this is to achieve elemental affinity between you (the occupant) with the energies of a particular floor.

As you are a Star 9 person of the Fire element, the chart below gives you the best floors for you to live on in terms of first choice, second choice, and third choice.

First Choice	Second Choice	Third Choice
2nd Floor	3rd Floor	4th Floor
7th Floor	8th Floor	9th Floor
12th Floor	13th Floor	14th Floor
17th Floor	18th Floor	19th Floor
22th Floor	23rd Floor	24th Floor
27th Floor	28th Floor	29th Floor
32th Floor	33th Floor	34th Floor
37th Floor	38th Floor	39th Floor
42th Floor	43rd Floor	44th Floor
47th Floor	48th Floor	49th Floor

Select :
Wood shaped buildings & Fire shaped buildings

Avoid :
Water shaped buildings & Earth shaped buildings

Personal Grand Duke Directions

Identifying the Grand Duke Sector is important. Your Personal Grand Duke Sector relates to your birth year. For example, if you are born in the year of the Rat then the Rat is your Personal Grand Duke and we know that the Rat sector is North 2.

We want to avoid the harmful properties of this area and as you are a Star 1 person, you can locate your Personal Grand Duke Sector in the following directions:

Personal Grand Duke Directions for Male

MALE Birth Year	Personal Grand Duke	Direction
1919, 1955, 1991, 2027	未 Wei Goat	西南1 Southwest 1
1928, 1964, 2000, 2036	辰 Chen Dragon	東南1 Southeast 1
1937, 1973, 2009, 2045	丑 Chou Ox	東北1 Northeast 1
1946, 1982, 2018, 2054	戌 Xu Dog	西北1 Northwest 1

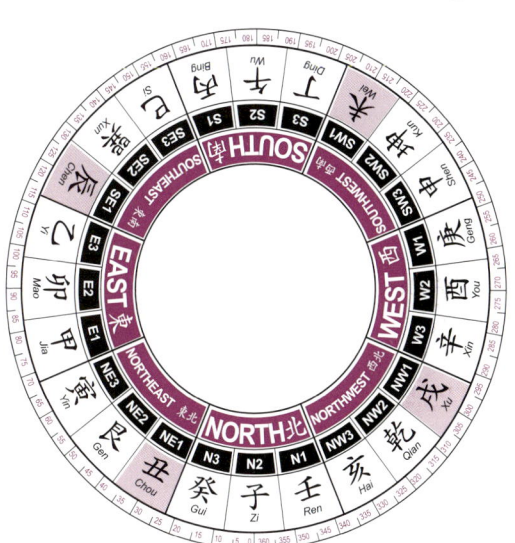

Personal Grand Duke Directions for Female

FEMALE Birth Year	Personal Grand Duke	Direction
1913, 1949, 1985, 2021	丑 Chou Ox	東北 1 Northeast 1
1922, 1958, 1994, 2030	戌 Xu Dog	西北 1 Northwest 1
1931, 1967, 2003, 2039	未 Wei Goat	西南 1 Southwest 1
1940, 1976, 2012, 2048	辰 Chen Dragon	東南 1 Southeast 1

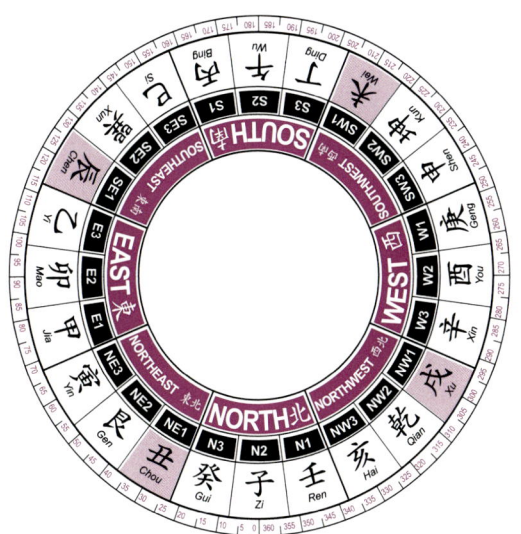

Ideally, you should not have a bathroom or toilet located in these areas of your home above and Sha Qi external features such as pylons, T-junctions, Dead Tree should be avoided. The Sha Qi in the Personal Grand Duke Sector is extremely strong and so all efforts to avoid spending a lot of time in it should be made. It goes without saying that the Personal Grand Duke Sector of your home is not the ideal spot for a bedroom! The Sha Qi in this area of the home is so strong in fact that it is difficult for any further negative Qi to enter!

Personal Clash Directions

Your home will contain Personal Clash Sectors. Spending time in these areas of your home will bring up problems in your life with significant others. As a Star 9 person, you will find your Personal Clash Sectors in the following directions:

Personal Clash Directions for Male

Personal Clash Directions

MALE Birth Year	Personal Clash Sector	Direction
1919, 1955, 1991, 2027	丑 Chou Ox	東北 1 Northeast 1
1928, 1964, 2000, 2036	戌 Xu Dog	西北 1 Northwest 1
1937, 1973, 2009, 2045	未 Wei Goat	西南 1 Southwest 1
1946, 1982, 2018, 2054	辰 Chen Dragon	東南 1 Southeast 1

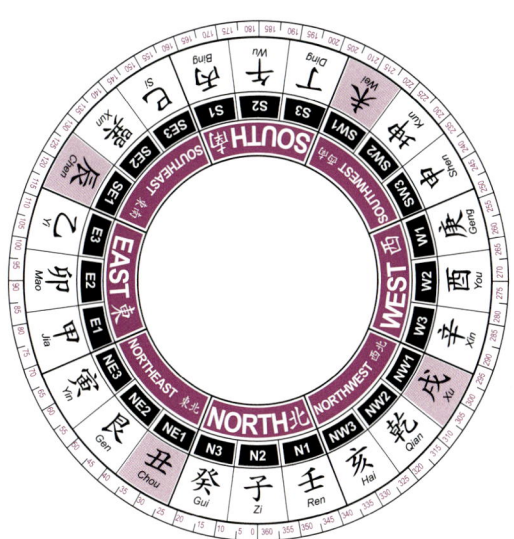

Personal Clash Directions for Female

FEMALE Birth Year	Personal Grand Duke	Direction
1913, 1949, 1985, 2021	未 Wei Goat	西南1 Southwest 1
1922, 1958, 1994, 2030	辰 Chen Dragon	東南1 Southeast 1
1931, 1967, 2003, 2039	丑 Chou Ox	東北1 Northeast 1
1940, 1976, 2012, 2048	戌 Xu Dog	西北1 Northwest 1

The locations above are a bad place for important features of your home such as the main door, bedroom and kitchen. You should seek to avoid these sectors in the same way you avoid your Personal Grand Duke Sector.

Flying Stars Effects

Each year, the Xuan Kong Flying Stars fly into a different section of a property, be it your residence or your work space. The effects that these Nine Stars have on you will be different depending on your Life Star. In this section you can find out how different Flying Stars in different sectors will effect you with regards to Feng Shui.

The Flying Stars have both negative and positive attributes, but which facets will show when you see a particular Star, depends on the timeliness and the period.

A few of the Nine Stars are inherently negative, a few are inherently positive in nature and some can be both good and bad. Even then, we must remember that the Stars have the capacity to manifest either their positive or negative facets because in Feng Shui, nothing is ever inherently bad or good forever.

When it comes to Flying Stars, it is important to remember this key principle: Forms activate the Stars and the Stars in turn influence the People. This is what you should keep in mind as you read about the effects of the Nine Stars on your Life Star.

1 ★ → 9 Purple Life

The effects of the visiting #1 White Star on a 9 Purple Life:

In terms of Feng Shui effects, the presence of the #1 White Star will bring about good academic luck and results. This is because scholarly activities derive benefits from the energies of Star #1. If you are sitting for an exam in the near future or writing a thesis, taking advantage of #1 White will yield great benefits for you. However, if there are negative external features present in the sector then #1 White brings about the risk of illness and poor health. When its negative influence manifests itself, #1 White also lead to romantic problems and issues. It does not bode well for you if you're in the midst of changing jobs or seeking out a new one.

2★ → 9 Purple Life

The effects of the visiting **#2 Black Star** on a 9 Purple Life:

In terms of Feng Shui effects, the presence of #2 Black brings undesirable results, particularly for women. Gynecological health issues are likely to arise because of the influence of #2 Black. Where possible, this is a combination that needs to be guarded against. It is particularly dangerous for pregnant women, as it could result in harmful complications.

4★ → 9 Purple Life

The effects of the visiting #4 Green Star on a 9 Purple Life:

In terms of Feng Shui effects, the presence of the #4 Green is likely to bring out of the ordinary events to pass. The chance of new sexual relations is increased so if you're married or in a relationship you need to guard against the effects of the #4 Green. If the external Feng Shui factors are good, however, then the #4 Green will bring about good health prospects. You will be able to recover from illnesses that do afflict you quickly and enjoy rejuvenating energy and a sense of wellbeing.

6★ → 9 Purple Life

The effects of the visiting **#6 White Star** on a 9 Purple Life:

In terms of Feng Shui effects, the presence of the #6 White brings about ill health. This can be quite serious, depending on whether or not there are negative structures outside of the sector. Health problems affecting the brain are possible. You could also suffer from issues affecting the lungs. When symptoms arise, you should not ignore them. You will leave yourself particularly open to issues if you smoke, such as bronchitis. Get any kind of persistent cough checked out as soon as possible.

7★ → 9 Purple Life

The effects of the visiting **#7 Red Star** on a 9 Purple Life:

In terms of Feng Shui effects, the presence of the #7 Red functions as a fire hazard, particularly if there are negative external factors outside the sector. Be careful with the wiring and switches in this area, as faulty wiring and electronics are the cause of many preventable fires! This combination will not be good for Star 9 people with heart issues or cardiac complications. If you have a weak heart or have a family history of heart problems, it will be best to avoid using this area.

8★ → 9 Purple Life

The effects of the visiting **#8 White Star** on a **9 Purple Life**:

In terms of Feng Shui effects, the presence of the #8 White could be good for romance, particularly for newly-married couples or older couples who have been together for a long time. You will find that it brings about harmonious relations and a general sense of happiness that contributes to both your wellbeing. In general, the #8 White brings about good events for most people, or at the very least, it improves your mood and promotes feelings of stability and happiness.

9★ → 9 Purple Life

The effects of the visiting **#9 Purple Star** on a **9 Purple Life**:

In terms of Feng Shui effects, the presence of the #9 Purple can clash with your own Life Star putting you on the edge, ready to explode. This is brought about by an excess of the Fire element. For some Star 9 people, the presence of #9 Purple could result in problems with eyesight or the eyes in general. However, it can still serve as a boon for financial development, and may bring about opportunities for increased wealth. It is also a very auspicious Star for the fashion and cosmetics industries.

五行

THE FIVE ELEMENTS

The Five Elements

The element of your Life Star 9 is Fire, and it is important that you understand the implications of this. In the study of Chinese Metaphysics and Feng Shui, a basic understanding of the Five Elements is integral to success. This section will briefly outline the role of the Five Elements.

The Five Elements are symbolic representations of energy, or Qi. In Feng Shui and in BaZi, the Five Elements are Earth, Metal, Water, Wood, and Fire. Fire represents warmth and expression, and like the heat emanated from the sun or a candle it denotes energy and inspiration as well as generosity and benevolence.

In order to understand the elements, it's important to understand their relationship to one another. Each element does not exist in isolation. As such, these elements share three important relationships known as 'cycles' that are fundamental to the understanding of Feng Shui: the Productive Cycle, the Controlling Cycle, and the Weakening Cycle.

Productive Cycle

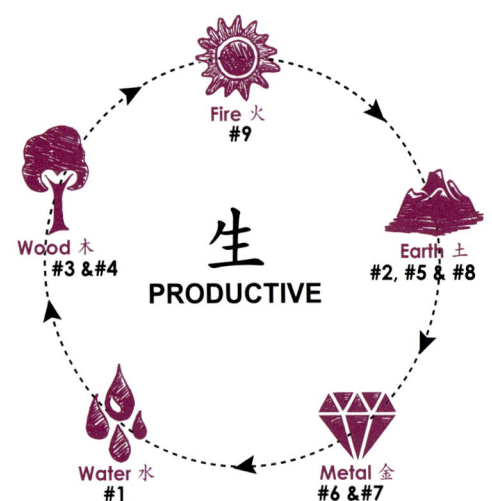

In this cycle,

Water produces Wood
Wood produces Fire
Fire produces Earth
Earth produces Metal
Metal produces Water

This is a cycle where the elements "produce" one another in terms of providing or helping the growth of another. In the case of Water, then, it produces nourishment for trees and plants (i.e. Wood). An element that produces another element means that it strengthens and grows the element that it produces. Here are some simple metaphors might help you visualize this better:

Water waters soil, producing Wood
Wood makes kindling, producing Fire
Fire makes ashes, producing Earth
Earth is mined, producing Metal
Metal melts, producing Water

Controlling Cycle

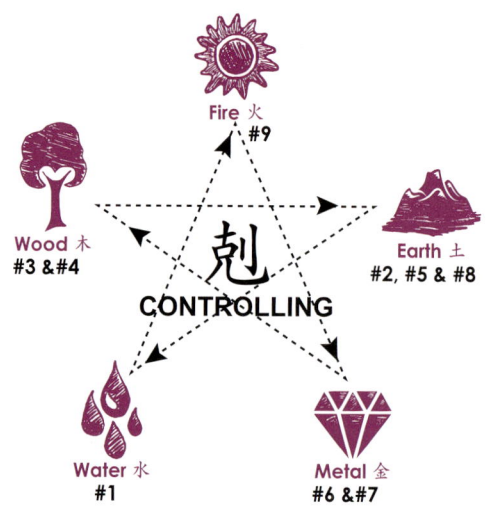

In this cycle,

Fire controls Metal
Metal controls Wood
Wood controls Earth
Earth controls Water
Water controls Fire

This is a cycle where the elements keep each under in "control": an element is countered or subjugated by its controlling element. In this instance, for example, the element of Water controls Fire by putting it out. Here are some simple metaphors to help you visualize it better:

Water extinguishes Fire
Fire melts Metal
Metal cuts Wood
Wood roots tightly grip Earth
Earth contains Water

Weakening Cycle

Fire 火
#9

Wood 木
#3 & #4

洩
WEAKENING

Earth 土
#2, #5 & #8

Water 水
#1

Metal 金
#6 & #7

In this cycle,

Water weakens Metal
Metal weakens Earth
Earth weakens Fire
Fire weakens Wood
Wood weakens Water

The Weakening Cycle can be best understood as the reverse of the Productive Cycle, in that the strength of the element is weakened by another in order to keep it in check. Remember, the key to Qi in Feng Shui is balance, and different elements keep other elements from becoming too strong. For example, Wood absorbs Water and therefore weakens it. Again, here are some metaphors for easier visualization:

Water can be partly absorbed by Wood
Wood can be partly burnt by Fire
Fire can be diminished with Earth
Earth is weakened when mined for Metal
Metal is corroded by Water

The following table shows you the Annual Stars for the year 2000 to 2026.

Examine it and figure out where your room lies; in which sector. Take note of the element of that sector and remember that as a Star 9 person, your element is Fire.

These Annual Stars shows you the location of the Stars in a property for the duration of the years specified. Based on the year, the Annual Stars will be located in different sectors of the house. Accordingly, different Annual Stars will affect the Feng Shui of your room in different years.

If the Annual Star of your bedroom is of the same element as your Life Star then the outcome is likely to be prosperous (Productive Cycle). If the Annual Star is your Life Star's controlling element (Controlling Cycle), then the result is likely to be stressful – although this combination is still desirable. But if the Annual Star element is the countering element (Countering Cycle) of your Life Star, then the combination is an unfavorable or inauspicious one for you. (Special note: the #5 Yellow Star is generally an undesirable Annual Star for your bedroom regardless of your Life Star.)

Think about the way the element of the Annual Star and your element (Fire) interact.

Besides the Annual Stars of the year, there also other factors to be considered. These include the Flying Stars chart of your specific house or property with the Sitting and Facing Stars. Advanced students may want to read *Xuan Kong Flying Stars Feng Shui* for further information. These Stars also affect the evaluation of the impact of the Xuan Kong Flying Stars on your property. There are many other ways of assessing the Feng Shui of a property, and it's important to understand that all these factors play an important and related role.

Characteristics of Star 9

We all have our "good days" and "bad days". Feng Shui seeks to help isolate why this happens and provide advice that you can use to make every day a "good day" where you are in your element. This section outlines the good and bad characteristics of your Life Star. In a positive sector of your house or work, the positive attributes of your Life Star will be further enhanced, and you will display more of these characteristics. In a negative sector, the positive attributes will be diminished and the negative attributes will begin to show through. Your bad characteristics will take center stage.

The Good

Inspiring

Out of all the Life Stars, Star 9 people, being of the Fire element, possess the spark that can light the fire of inspiration, be it for yourself or for others. You tend to be self-motivated and you can inspire the same motivation in those around you. You find ways to root for the underdog and your enthusiastic interest and contributions to the projects of others helps get them off the ground. As such, others tend to like having you around.

Driven

You can be very driven and ambitious, particularly if something has captured your imagination. Once committed, you are a perfectionist who likes to ensure that every detail is present and correct and that everything goes according to plan. Once you take on something, you have to see it through the end till it is done properly.

Generous

The Star 9 character tends to be particularly generous and benevolent. You may be actively involved in some forms of charity but even if this not the case you will always readily give your advice, love, and time to others who need it. At your best you can be fundamentally selfless and nurturing. You will not hold back or be calculative.

Spontaneous

Some people may see you as being impetuous, but you are generally someone who is spontaneous and does things in the spur-of-the-moment. Like a candle flame, you can be blown around by the slightest breeze. You are not rigid and unyielding to sudden changes in your plan. The outcome of this is that you are prone to doing new things as the situation around you changes. At your best, this means that you are capable of reacting with aplomb to any sudden changes or diversions in plan.

壞

The Bad

Mercurial

As a Fire element Star, you can be changeable and hard to pin down. At an unhealthy level, this means that you can often be mercurial and volatile, depending on how the wind blows. This is when others have a hard time knowing what you're going to do, or when you yourself are not sure what you're going to do. Being fickle minded means that you may start on something today and abandon it tomorrow, or make poorly thought out commitments that you are then unable to follow up on.

Hasty

You can make decisions in a hasty and impatient manner. This is largely tied to your predilection to be mercurial when in an unhealthy state of mind; you simply can't wait to make a decision! Being too impatient and rushing through important decisions means that you overlook difficulties and problems which later crop up and cause you trouble.

Dependent

Like a flame that needs air to exist, Star 9 people can become too reliant on others to get things done. This means that you constantly feel the need to be bathed in the the attention or focus of other people before you can get started on a project or even complete a goal. This, in a sense, is a paradox – while you're able to motivate others, you can also slide into an existence where you wait for others to motivate you. If nobody is taking notice, you reason, then why bother?

Superficial

Your excitement and enthusiasm is attractive. It can endow others with passion for things you are involved in. You can appear to have brilliant ideas on the surface, but when people press you for hard details, they can discover that you have not properly thought through your ideas. You become quickly engrossed in something and tend to skip a lot of important groundwork in the race to reach the finish line.

職業和財富

CAREER AND WEALTH

Characteristics at Work

As a Star 9 person, you may display some of these basic characteristics in professional situations at the workplace and in relation to your career. Being aware of your own key characteristics will help you understand why you act and react to situations, people, and tasks in the way you do.

This section outlines the good and bad characteristics of your Life Star. In a positive sector of your house or work, the positive attributes of your Life Star will be further enhanced, and you will display more of these characteristics. In a negative sector, the positive attributes will be diminished and the negative attributes will begin to show through. Your bad characteristics will take center stage.

• Perfectionist

You are someone who is always keen to get the details right, and sometimes you may appear nitpicky to those around you. But, perfectionism – to an extent - is a good trait to cultivate on the job, because if you don't pay attention to the details then no one else will. Sometimes you tend to focus too much on the surface of things, however, and you can become so enamored with a relatively insignificant detail that larger ones remain unattended to. Prioritize.

- ## Passionate

As a Star 9 person at work, you distinguish yourself with the passion you bring to your projects and tasks. Your energy and enthusiasm for the things that capture your interest render you a valuable team player at the office. These qualities make you the kind of employee that employers typically dream of finding. If you're leading a department, this passion filters down to those under you, producing superior results.

- ## Supportive

Your generous, benevolent nature goes down well at the work place, because you provide a crucial supporting role in terms of providing assistance and guidance. More often

than not, people also turn to you as a sort of mentor, and this enables you to form wide ranging social connections at work. Your sociable and friendly nature only helps you to become more popular still.

• Problem-solving

When a problem arises you don't lose your cool and stand waving your arms in dismay – you take a step back, assess the situation, and begin strategically figuring out a solution. Your approach to solving problems is not haphazard and so your success rate in solving problems is high!

Suitable Job Roles

• Artist, performing arts

Success as an artist or in the performing arts depends upon the ability to perform and express emotions, both of which you can do. You look at things from a variety of angles in your efforts to make sense of them, and very often the insight you gain from this process comes out in the form of artistic expression. You have a desire to show your talents to the world and to draw attention to your abilities, and performance plays perfectly to these needs. You possess an inner drive that will be necessary for an artist who may have to struggle for a long time before attaining the recognition they deserve.

- ## Actor, model, entertainment industry

You are charming, charismatic, and gregarious, and tend to have an extroverted nature. You express yourself without much provocation! As such, you will do well in job roles that require you to express yourself and take center-stage in the spotlight. Your natural charisma is the X-factor here; it makes others want to stop and pay attention to you. People either have natural charisma or they don't. It cannot be taught. Fortunately, you possess it!

- ## Television, radio announcer

You will also be good in a role that requires you to project your attention outward, and towards others. As an announcer on the television or the radio, the impetus

will be on you to keep people tuned in and your charm and friendly manner of speech make you the perfect candidate for the job. Your ability to interact with others and convey information succinctly is a definite plus here. You will also have your own opinions and stance on the issues you are reporting on which can sometimes be called upon in certain styles of reporting.

• Design, beauty industries

You will do well in these fields, as well, because you care about aesthetics and have a good idea of how to make things and people look better. You are adept at dealing with the public, and have a quick, sharp mind which means that you can handle the business side of things. Being a great designer is all fine and well but when you add an entrepreneurial spin into the mix you have a recipe for a rewarding career.

Career and Wealth Guide

- # Focus on the external

Too often, you approach things with yourself in mind. You think how events will pan out from your perspective and how they will serve you. In short, you can be too self absorbed. Although you are helpful to others and nurturing, your professional networks and alliances will become better if you know how to empathize and put yourself in the shoes of others. Once you have an idea of how things affect others you can ingratiate yourself by making sure you do things that please those around you and generate results for them. What goes around comes around, after all.

- **Channel your flamboyance wisely**

  It's all well and good to seek affirmation for your efforts and to enjoy attention, but not all attention is necessarily good attention. At work, you will have to be careful that the attention you focus on yourself doesn't detract from the focus that people should be paying to your work and actual accomplishments and talents. Don't become too attached to the ideas of attention and spectacle.

- ## Delve deep

More often than not, you get hung up on the surface details. Explore the depths of it. If you only look at things briefly before making a decision you are not making decisions, properly. Change your approach so that you spend time on both content and appearance. Learn that you have a lot to learn from others, instead of always assuming that you have something to teach them.

- # Be more independent

Particularly where your wealth generating attempts are concerned, it will not be wise to merely rely on what others tell you or suggest you do with your money. Read up on good investment practices and do your own research so that you can independently evaluate opportunities and potential reasonably. If you're too dependent on the opinions of others, you can easily be led astray or cast adrift.

• Learn to accept criticism

You tend to be prickly and defensive when it comes to criticism from others, and this is in large part because you don't like to be told what you're doing wrong, even if you can see where others are coming from. It will be crucial to learn to really take what other people say to you on board. Pay attention to constructive criticism because in the long run it's good for you.

Famous Personalities :

Bill Gates
Bill Clinton
Steven Spielberg
Donald Trump

人際關係

RELATIONSHIPS

Guide for Relationships

As a Star 9 person, you typically do not have a problem drawing other people into your orbit. You possess a certain beauty made up of warmth and brilliance that draws other people in. You are opinionated and you express these opinions in a passionate way. People find your enthusiasm for things that capture your interest infectious and exciting. As such, you don't really have a problem with meeting and attracting people and falling into relationships.

In general, if you and your partner have mutual admiration and respect, it is fairly easy for you to keep the relationship going. Depending on your personality, you tend to have either very liberal or very conservative views about sexual relations, and depending on where you fall it will be important that you convey your thoughts and feelings on the matter quite adequately to your partner to avoid any misunderstandings. If you don't bring things out into the open when it comes to the bedroom, resentment or fear can build up.

You tend to seek out people who have quick, sharp minds like yours but you find it hard to settle down for the long-term with those who have opinions diametrically opposed to yours. This is because you become quite opinionated yourself and you prefer an audience willing to easily embrace your strong views instead of someone who will constantly challenge you on them!

Out of all the Stars, Star 9 people tend to have the most significant problems adjusting to the demands of marriage. You do struggle to view the marriage as a union of two people rather than an arrangement made to benefit you. You have difficulty transferring the focus from yourself to your spouse. This is not because you're inherently selfish, it's just that you have become accustomed to thinking of things from your perspective and so when you are thrust into marriage you must make a conscious effort to consider things from multiple perspectives. Also, you subscribe to the notion that you should be able to have 'fun' whenever you want to, and a marriage and family quickly puts this to an end.

Star 9 in relationships:

Star 9 people tend to base their judgments on external appearances. They often receive romantic invitations, but may get into trouble if they arc not careful.

健康

HEALTH

Guide for Health

Body parts and organs that are related to Star 9: Heart, lungs, small and large intestine.

The Star 9 individual has a pretty robust immune system and enjoys good health. Consequently, you're generally blessed with good energy. However, if you do fall ill, you can expect any symptoms or diseases to be ones involving the organs associated with your Star. Pay attention to any changes in your heart rate or rhythm because heart problems are the most mortal threat that a Star 9 person faces with regards too their health. If you're older and with an already diagnosed heart condition then it will be important to follow all your doctor's instructions closely.

Further related health problems include strokes and high or low blood pressure. In your general day-to-day life, you may fall sick easily. Colds and flu are old friends of yours but they vanish as soon as they come, barely affecting you at all. However, when you do fall seriously ill, the situation must be treated with a sense of gravity. Lessen the pace of your activities, calm your energy and focus on healing and recovery.

You also tend to have eye problems quite frequently, and it would be prudent to have frequent eye examinations to rule out any developing conditions. As you get older, you will be more prone to arthritis. Finally, in general, maintain a careful diet, as constipation and diarrhea could be recurring problems if you simply eat whatever you want, whenever you want.

Potential health concerns:

Eye-related problems
Heart attack & stroke
Blood-related ailments
Paralysis
Temperamental behavior

COMPATIBILITY WITH OTHER LIFE STARS

This section examines your compatibility as a Star 9 person with other people who have the same and different Stars. No person goes through life completely alone. Relationships with others form the bedrock of good career networking. Friendships and relations with loved ones, spouses, partners and family make everything worth while. It is necessary to understand how compatible people with different Stars are to prevent conflict and missed opportunities. Bear in mind that issues of compatibility are not definite or set in stone. There are exceptions to every rule. In addition, **the quality of Feng Shui** in your environment helps dictate whether positive or negative traits in people manifest themselves and thus it weighs in on the quality of your relationships with those people. This section serves as a good guide on your relationships with other people of different Stars.

Star 9 people tend to either get along either really well or really poorly with fellow Star 9 people. You can either work productively together towards shared long term goals or you could find yourselves clashing with one another. When dealing with Star 1 people, you should pay attention to what's going on and remain alert, as Star 1 is of the Water element

and Water counters Fire, and you could be on the losing end of any interactions with them.

Your relationship with people of Stars 3 and 4 is likely to be very good as they tend to be patient and being around them will be beneficial to you. They tend to be the people who support and help you along. Similarly, with people of Stars 6 and 7, there is likely to be good affinity be it in a personal or professional capacity.

Where people of Stars 2, 5, and 8 are concerned, you need to tread wisely as these Stars are of the Earth element, and Fire produces Earth becoming weaker in the process. Because of this, there is a likelihood that long-term relationships will be problematic, particularly in terms of a long-term business partnership. It is probably best that you do not get involved with Star 5 individuals because things will end partIcularIty badly.

The chart below lists element people or sectors you can utilize to improve your compatibility with other Star people.

	Compatibility with others Stars (Individuals)	Seek help from this element people or use this sector
Star 9	Stars 2, 5 & 8 (Earth Element)	Fire
	Stars 3 & 4 (Wood Element)	Water
	Stars 6 & 7 (Metal Element)	Earth
	Star 9 (Fire Element)	Metal
	Star 1 (Water Element)	Wood

巽 SE Xun	離 S Li	坤 SW Kun
4 Green WOOD	**9** Purple FIRE	**2** Black EARTH
3 Jade WOOD	**5** Yellow EARTH	**7** Red METAL
8 White EARTH	**1** White WATER	**6** White METAL
艮 NE Gen	坎 N Kan	乾 NW Qian

震 E Zhen   兑 W Dui

The following pages will explain in detail the compatibility factor of a Star 9 person with people of all other nine Stars through the Compatibility Meter. The Compatibility Guides give you tips for managing the relationships in question.

| **9** Purple | compatibility with | **1** White |

Compatibility Meter

When you and a Star 1 person get together, the outcome will be complicated. You will probably find that social interactions hold your interest. Star 1 people are famously good at socializing with all other types of people, being highly adaptive. This can lull you into a false sense of security and perhaps make a business partnership seem like a good idea. After all, Star 1 people are intelligent and creative and together you can generate results. They may be able to help temper your vague plans and turn your broadly sketched out ideas into more tangible ones. They will see holes in plans that you will skim over. Having said all of this, a business partnership may not be such a good idea. In terms of who comes out on top as a result of your interactions, it is likely that you will end up losing out in the long term. This may not necessarily be a problem

until you start putting money down based on the strength of your relationship! You are selfless and Star 1 individuals are known to have a manipulative streak which they will use to get ahead of you, leaving you behind once they've done so. Friendships will go over smoothly and so, be extension will romantic partnerships so it may be better to keep your connections with Star 1 people personal in nature. When all is said and done, the basic attraction between Star 9 and Star 1 people is strong on many levels so that any conflict between you always ends in reconciliation and forgiveness.

Compatibility Guide

When you get together with a Star 1 person, you need to be extra careful if it is a partnership. Where professional interaction, trading, and business are concerned, you can often be the one who comes out on the losing end because Star 1's Water element counters your Fire element. You must be alert to all that is taking place. In a friendship or a romance, consideration will be the key factor – try to think of the other person every once in a while. If you do not reassure them they are likely to remain distant.

| 9 Purple | compatibility with | 2 Black |

Compatibility Meter

When you and a Star 2 person get together, there is the potential for affinity.

While in the long run the Star 2 person may prove to have a weakening effect on you, the relationship is not necessarily going to be a bad one. In this case, the weakening effect comes about in a different way. Because Star 2 people are passive and calm and tranquil, they can serve to "extinguish" the more fiery parts of your nature. Spending time around them will mellow you out somewhat and without your energy you will not be as successful in your pursuits. Although they are dedicated and practical and may have their use in shaping your ideas into realistic plans, they will, truth be told, put a dampener on your enthusiasm for a project. They are best suited to work as employees

rather than direct partners for this reason. In relationships, Star 2 people are very sentimental when it comes to romance so you must try and live up to their expectations. This means you must think about what will make them happy and make a sefless effort to do so.

Compatibility Guide

In this connection, you need to consider if a long-term partnership is worth it and beneficial to you. Star 2 is of the Earth element, and it can weaken your Fire element. Where a friendship or romance is concerned, you have to be the one to play it cool instead of "over-caring", or showing too much interest, as the Star 2 person will quickly retreat and possibly walk away. Bear in mind that if the Star 2 person needs your help, they will ask for it – don't be excessively helpful or you will be used or taken for granted.

| **9** Purple | compatibility with | **3** Jade |

Compatibility Meter

When you and a Star 3 person get together, the outcome will be lots of fun! You will find that they are active and energetic and that they live life at an urgent pace which makes them intrinsically interesting to be around. You and the Star 3 person tend to be similarly enthusiastic about the same things, and also tend to be very emotionally expressive and articulate. As such, in a friendship or relationship there is the worry that the relationship might be formed over superficial affinities instead of any real foundational bond. You may find that you build a superficial bond, easily broken. At work, you share many of the same counterproductive traits which may make a partnership inadvisable. For example, Star 3 people are rash. They rush into things. When you consider that you – in

your excitement to begin a new project – are prone to glazing over the important details, you can see how glaring problems can be ignored until it is too late.

Compatibility Guide

While there will be great affinity with you and the Star 3 person, for something meaningful to develop, some intervention is called for. If you do not make an effort to bond, all of your interactions are done from behind a social mask of sorts. To go beyond being fair-weather friends, or people who get together only for a good time, you might need to sit down for a heart to heart in order to break through the social faces you both wear! This is particularly true if you're establishing a romantic relationship. It will be imperative to get to know each others values, principles, and thoughts before any progress can be made. Involve a third pary in your decision making processes if working together to help introduce some caution so that you do not rush into things.

| **9** Purple | compatibility with | **4** White |

Compatibility Meter

When you and a Star 4 person get together, the result is likely to be good.

There is likely to be mutual affection and between you and the Star 4 person, and both will enjoy being given the time and space to show each other their talents. Star 4 people are highly creative and you will appreciate their soft nature during your interactions with them as you tend to shy away from loud, obnoxious types. The mutual sharing and admiration of each others abilities will be the glue that keeps the relationship or friendship going. You will come to appreciate each other's artistic endeavors! You may encounter some issues at work if this is a business partnership or a colleague. Because Star 4 individuals find it hard to settle down and commit to a plan, they may begin to go off on

a tangent when they really ought to stick to an agreed course of action! Romantically, they can become clingy and dependent when not at their best which can scare you off.

Compatibility Guide

In order to make this work, it should be noted that both Star 9 and Star 4 people must first try to be on the same wavelength, or that they must have the same goals. A partnership is likely to go awry if both carry on in separate ways towards different things, simply because both of you are opinionated and have confidence in your own talent. While Star 4 people might be soft spoken, they are strong underneath – just like you – and are not easily manipulated or controlled. You may have to be the more decisive one in this partnership, because the Star 4 person can be indecisive and paranoid at times. This poses a challenge for you but being decisive doesn't mean being aggressive or confrontational; you can still steer things along with a gentle hand.

| **9** Purple | compatibility with | **5** Yellow |

Compatibility Meter

Interactions between a Star 9 individual and a Star 5 individual are unlikely to yield desirable results. There is likely to be some form of care, but it will largely come in modest doses which don't propel the connection forward. Partnerships are best avoided, as losses can afflict you in particular, and not so much the Star 5 person. They are calculative, with a definite agenda, and you are unlikely to be aware of this until they have used you and are ready to move on. In a relationship, there is a risk of a break-up as well as the Star 5 person is bound to feel stressed with your emotional tendencies. They are independent and strong and will expect the same from you. When you show that your feelings or that you need them, they will only seek escape and behave in a distant manner.

Compatibility Guide

This is probably a connection that is best kept at a surface level, since giving too much of your care and help may only exhaust you and lead you astray. It depends a lot on the Star 5 personality. If your instincts tell you that the person can be trusted, then you can slowly offer more of your assistance bit by bit. Approach all matters of finance with caution. Avoid your inclination to rush in and make sure you fully explore all avenues before making decisions that can leave you open to losses.

| **9** Purple | compatibility with | **6** White |

Compatibility Meter

When you and Star 6 person get together, you can expect a positive outcome in most cases. There is likely to be good synergy between the Star 9 and the Star 6 individual. Both of you possess frank and engaging personalities, and the two of you also work at the same energy level! As such, your communication is likely to be smooth. On a personal level, you can do a lot of good for the Star 6 person. You are fiery yet caring and you can penetrate the shield which Star 6 people build around themselves. They live a noble yet isolated life and even if they do not immediately show it, they will appreciate your efforts to get to know them. The passion and enthusiasm you show for things you are involved in will register with them as they have similar enthusiasm for matters close to the heart. They do not take a quiet stance when they feel they have something to say!

Compatibility Guide

One possible avenue for conflict exists because of your habit of changing your point of view on issues. Star 6 people have concrete ideas of what is correct and incorrect and if you constantly shift your position on things then by definition you will sometimes disagree and sometimes agree with them. If they get the idea in their head that you are fickle they can begin to lose respect for you. While your relationship will largely be a smooth one, you can certainly help it along! It will be necessary to cultivate compassion and tolerance, instead of always expecting the Star 6 person to cede to your opinion. Most of all, don't use your emotions as a benchmark for your reactions. Strive to be rational and thoughtful, and the Star 6 person will appreciate this deeply.

9 Purple compatibility with 7 Red

Compatibility Meter

When you get together with a Star 7 person, there is bound to be mutual attraction. You are outgoing and loud and this means that wherever you go you are a great asset to any social situation. Star 7 people thrive on great conversation and the finer things in life and you will click when you meet. You may even feel a strong initial spark of chemistry. You are genuine and you take an interest in others and they have a strong need for attention. Since you will give them this attention, they will want to keep you around because it makes them feel good! There will be ample opportunity for warmth and cordiality to form through the ability of you and the Star 7 person to express your feelings. However, there will also be friction quite frequently due to warring egos and a tendency for both of you to need

attention from the other. You require that other people take note of the things you achieve whilst Star 7 people are only ever happy when people appreciate who they are and shower them with praise.

Compatibility Guide

As can be said of your relationship to the Star 6 person, there is likely to be easy, mutual attraction that helps things along. But there will be occasional simmering tension brought upon by differing opinions and this will be the crucial moment where it will be important for you to deal with it with grace. In arguments with the Star 7 person, discuss facts of the disagreement and don't point your finger in order to assign blame. If you can learn how to handle the disagreements that arise between you then all is well. You must also not fall into the trap of existing solely to give them attention. Make sure you get some benefit in kind from the time you spend with them.

| **9** Purple | compatibility with | **8** White |

Compatibility Meter

When Star 9 people get together with Star 8 people, there is likely to be a good professional connection. You and the Star 8 person tend to have similar professional goals, and are also mutually-admiring of each others talents. Like two halves of a circle, your strengths and weaknesses interlock to produce a strong overall whole. You are enthusiastic and passionate whilst they are cool and reserved. They are cautious whilst you are rash. Together you can hit some kind of middle ground where things get done and opportunities aren't missed. Therefore, this is likely to be a highly-productive and beneficial professional relationship. On a personal level, friendship is still possible but may be more hard to come by. You are outgoing and expressive whilst they are anything but! In fact, they rarely ever express any feelings

about anything, even if they do hold feelings inside. It may be up to you to coax them out of their shell.

Compatibility Guide

In a business venture or partnership of some sort, it will be important to outline the roles that the both of you play, and to observe your behavior in line with those roles. Don't stray from tasks and duties you have been assigned because this will not please the Star 8 person. Although it is unlikely that they will explode into a fit of rage when you step out of line or fail to perform they will take note of it and eventually you may find that they will stop giving you chances, being themselves dependable and thus expecting this trait in others. They may find your expressiveness somewhat overwhelming or off-putting if they think that you are chaotic or messy. Work hard, deliver on promises and slowly gain their trust.

	compatibility with	
9 Purple		**9** Purple

Compatibility Meter

When you and a Star 9 person come together, the outcome is hard to call. On a personal level, you are both warm and caring so your interactions will be smooth and unproblematic when you first meet. The problems that may develop step from your mercurial nature. You can change your mind at the drop of a hat and so a good thing can turn sour very quickly! In a partnership, knowing each other's strengths and weaknesses can be an added advantage in tackling work demands and goals together. You will both be enthusiastic about anything you are involved in and there will not be power struggles but you will also both be tempted to rush forward too quickly. Romantically, you will find each other's quick wit attractive. In the long term, however, marriage may not be advisable as you will

both have a hard time adjusting and you may find that both of you spend the majority of the time thinking of yourselves. Hardly conducive to domestic bliss!

Compatibility Guide

In a negative frame of mind, you and the other Star 9 can both be opinionated, impetuous, emotional, and hasty – and as such need to strive to be more humble and modest in dealings with each other. Otherwise any partnership is bound to only be an exhausting clash of egos. This will be true regardless of a friendship, romance, or professional relationship. You may well need to enlist the help of someone who has a different Life Star when drawing up plans and coming up with ideas. You come up with good ideas but once you have something you think you'd like to run with, you run! You need someone there to tell you when things are unrealistic or flawed and when two Star 9 people work together in isolation this will not happen.

About Joey Yap

Joey Yap first began learning about Chinese Metaphysics from masters in the field when he was fifteen.

Despite having graduated with a Commerce degree in Accounting, Joey never became an accountant. Instead, he began to give seminars, talks and professional Chinese Metaphysic consultations in Malaysia, Singapore, India, Australia, Canada, England, Germany and the United States, becoming a household name in the field.

By the age of twenty-six, Joey became a self-made millionaire and in 2008, he was listed in The Malaysian Tatler as the Top 300 Most Influential People in Malaysia and Prestige's Top 40 Under 40.

His practical and result-driven take on Feng Shui and BaZi sets him apart from other older, traditional masters and practitioners in the field. He shows people how the ancient teachings can be utilized for tangible REAL world benefits. The success he and his clients enjoy, thanks to his advice, is positive proof that Feng Shui and BaZi Astrology works, whether everyone believes in it or not!

Today, Joey has helped and worked with governments and the wealthiest people in Singapore, Hong Kong, China, Malaysia and Japan. His clients include multinationals, developers, tycoons and royalties. On Bloomberg, he is featured on-air as a regular guest on the subject of Feng Shui annual forecasts. He is retained by twenty-five top Malaysian property developers to help determine suitable candidates to take top management, change their space and Feng Shui mechanism, the way they make decisions, and understand the natural cosmic energies that can influence their decision-making.

Every year he conducts his 'Feng Shui and Astrology' seminar to a crowd of more than 3500 people at the Kuala Lumpur Convention Center. He also takes this annual seminar on a world tour to Frankfurt, San Francisco, New York, Las Vegas, Toronto, Sydney and Singapore.

The Joey Yap Consulting Group is the world's largest and first specialized metaphysics consultation firm. His consultancy, and professional speaking and training engagements with Microsoft, HP, Bloomberg, Citibank, HSBC and many more have seen the benefits of Classical Feng Shui and BaZi find their way into corporate environment and culture. Celebrities, property developers and other large organizations turn to Joey when they need the best.

After years of field-testing and fine-tuning his teachings, he has put together a team in the form of Joey Yap Research International. The objective of this Research Team is to scientifically track and verify the positive impact of Feng Shui and BaZi on subjects and ultimately to assist more people in achieving their life goals.

The Mastery Academy of Chinese Metaphysics which Joey founded teaches thousands of students from all around the world about Classical Feng Shui, Chinese Astrology and Face Reading. Many graduates have gone on to become successful in their own right, becoming sought after consultants, setting up their own consultancy businesses or even becoming educators, passing on Chinese Metaphysics knowledge to others.

Joey has also created the Decision Referential Technology™, offering decision reformation training on how to make better decisions in business and in personal life. He has led his team of highly trained consultants to help clients create more positive change in corporate boardrooms and increase production in their companies, helping people see their business outlook for each year so they may anticipate, plan and execute their strategies successfully.

Joey's work has been featured regularly in various popular global publications and networks like Time, Forbes, the International Herald Tribune and Bloomberg. He has also written columns for The New Straits Times, The Star and The Edge – Malaysia's leading newspapers. He has achieved bestselling author status with over sixty-five books, which have sold more than three million copies to-date.

His success is not limited to matters of Feng Shui and BaZi. Although his success is a product of them, he is also a successful entrepreneur, leading his own companies and property investment portfolio. When not teaching metaphysics or consulting around the world, Joey is a Naruto-fan, avid snowboarder and is crazy for fruits de mer.

Author's personal website :

 www.joeyyap.com

Joey Yap on Facebook:

 www.facebook.com/JoeyYapFB

MASTERY ACADEMY
OF CHINESE METAPHYSICS
Your **Preferred** Choice to the Art & Science of Classical Chinese Metaphysics Studies

Bringing **innovative** techniques and **creative** teaching methods to an ancient study.

Mastery Academy of Chinese Metaphysics was established by Joey Yap to play the role of disseminating this Eastern knowledge to the modern world with the belief that this valuable knowledge should be accessible to anyone, anywhere.

Its goal is to enrich people's lives through accurate, professional teaching and practice of Chinese Metaphysics knowledge globally. It is the first academic institution of its kind in the world to adopt the tradition of Western institutions of higher learning - where students are encourage to explore, question and challenge themselves and to respect different fields and branches of study - with the appreciation and respect of classical ideas and applications that have stood the test of time.

The art and science of Chinese Metaphysics studies – be it Feng Shui, BaZi (Astrology), Mian Xiang (Face Reading), ZeRi (Date Selection) or Yi Jing – is no longer a field shrouded with mystery and superstition. In light of new technology, fresher interpretations and innovative methods as well as modern teaching tools like the Internet, interactive learning, e-learning and distance learning, anyone from virtually any corner of the globe, who is keen to master these disciplines can do so with ease and confidence under the guidance and support of the Academy.

It has indeed proven to be a center of educational excellence for thousands of students from over thirty countries across the world; many of whom have moved on to practice classical Chinese Metaphysics professionally in their home countries.

At the Academy, we believe in enriching people's lives by empowering their destinies through the disciplines of Chinese Metaphysics. Learning is not an option - it's a way of life!

MASTERY ACADEMY
OF CHINESE METAPHYSICS™

MALAYSIA
19-3, The Boulevard, Mid Valley City, 59200 Kuala Lumpur, Malaysia
Tel : +603-2284 8080 | Fax : +603-2284 1218
Email   : info@masteryacademy.com
Website : www.masteryacademy.com

Australia, Austria, Canada, China, Croatia, Cyprus, Czech Republic, Denmark, France, Germany, Greece, Hungary, India, Italy, Kazakhstan, Malaysia, Netherlands (Holland), New Zealand, Philippines, Poland, Russian Federation, Singapore, Slovenia, South Africa, Switzerland, Turkey, U.S.A., Ukraine, United Kingdom

www.masteryacademy.com | +603 - 2284 8080

Mastery Academy around the world

JOEY YAP CONSULTING GROUP

Pioneering Metaphysics - Centric Personal Coaching and Corporate Consulting

The Joey Yap Consulting Group is the world's first specialised metaphysics consultation firm. Founded in 2002 by renown international Feng Shui and BaZi consultant, author and trainer Joey Yap, the Joey Yap Consulting Group is a pioneer in the provision of metaphysics-driven coaching and consultation services for individuals and corporations.

The Group's core consultation practice areas are Feng Shui and BaZi, which are complimented by ancillary services like Date Selection, Face Reading and Yi Jing Divination. The Group's team of highly-trained professional consultants are led by Principal Consultant Joey Yap. The Joey Yap Consulting Group is the firm of choice for corporate captains, entrepreneurs, celebrities and property developers when it comes to Feng Shui and BaZi-related advisory and knowledge.

Across Industries: Our Portfolio of Clients

Our diverse portfolio of both corporate and individual clients from all around the world bears testimony to our experience and capabilities.

Joey Yap Consulting Group is the firm of choice for many of Asia's leading multi-national corporations, listed entities, conglomerates and top-tier property developers when it comes to Feng Shui and corporate BaZi.

Our services also engaged by professionals, prominent business personalities, celebrities, high-profile politicians and people from all walks of life.

JOEY YAP CONSULTING GROUP

Name (Mr./Mrs./Ms.):_____

Contact Details

Tel:_____ Fax:_____

Mobile :_____

E-mail:_____

What Type of Consultation Are You Interested In?
- [ ] Feng Shui - [ ] BaZi - [ ] Date Selection - [ ] Corporate Events

Please tick if applicable:
- [ ] Are you a Property Developer looking to engage Joey Yap Consulting Group?
- [ ] Are you a Property Investor looking for tailor-made packages to suit your investment requirements?

Please attach your name card here.

Thank you for completing this form. Please fax it back to us at:

Malaysia & the rest of the world
Fax : +603-2284 2213   Tel : +603-2284 1213

www.joeyyap.com

Feng Shui Consultations

For Residential Properties
- Initial Land/Property Assessment
- Residential Feng Shui Consultations
- Residential Land Selection
- End-to-End Residential Consultation

For Commercial Properties
- Initial Land/Property Assessment
- Commercial Feng Shui Consultations
- Commercial Land Selection
- End-to-End Commercial Consultation

For Property Developers
- End-to-End Consultation
- Post-Consultation Advisory Services
- Panel Feng Shui Consultant

For Property Investors
- Your Personal Feng Shui Consultant
- Tailor-Made Packages

For Memorial Parks & Burial Sites
- Yin House Feng Shui

BaZi Consultations

Personal Destiny Analysis
- Personal Destiny Analysis for Individuals
- Children's BaZi Analysis
- Family BaZi Analysis

Strategic Analysis for Corporate Organizations
- Corporate BaZi Consultations
- BaZi Analysis for Human Resource Management

Entrepreneurs & Business Owners
- BaZi Analysis for Entrepreneurs

Career Pursuits
- BaZi Career Analysis

Relationships
- Marriage and Compatibility Analysis
- Partnership Analysis

For Everyone
- Annual BaZi Forecast
- Your Personal BaZi Coach

Date Selection Consultations

- **Marriage Date Selection**
- **Caesarean Birth Date Selection**
- **House-Moving Date Selection**
- **Renovation & Groundbreaking Dates**

- **Signing of Contracts**
- **Official Openings**
- **Product Launches**

Corporate Events

Many reputable organizations and instituitions have worked closely with Joey Yap Consulting Group to build a synergistic business relationship by engaging our team of consultants, led by Joey Yap, as speakers at their corporate events.

We tailor our seminars and talks to suit the anticipated or pertinent group of audience. Be it department, subsidiary, your clients or even the entire corporation, we aim to fit your requirements in delivering the intended message(s).

Tel: +603-2284 1213   Email: consultation@joeyyap.com

Chinese Metaphysics Reference Series

The Chinese Metaphysics Reference Series is a collection of reference texts, source material, and educational textbooks to be used as supplementary guides by scholars, students, researchers, teachers and practitioners of Chinese Metaphysics.

These comprehensive and structured books provide fast, easy reference to aid in the study and practice of various Chinese Metaphysics subjects including Feng Shui, BaZi, Yi Jing, Zi Wei, Liu Ren, Ze Ri, Ta Yi, Qi Men and Mian Xiang.

The Chinese Metaphysics Compendium

At over 1,000 pages, the *Chinese Metaphysics Compendium* is a unique one-volume reference book that compiles all the formulas relating to Feng Shui, BaZi (Four Pillars of Destiny), Zi Wei (Purple Star Astrology), Yi Jing (I-Ching), Qi Men (Mystical Doorways), Ze Ri (Date Selection), Mian Xiang (Face Reading) and other sources of Chinese Metaphysics.

It is presented in the form of easy-to-read tables, diagrams and reference charts, all of which are compiled into one handy book. This first-of-its-kind compendium is presented in both English and the original Chinese, so that none of the meanings and contexts of the technical terminologies are lost.

The only essential and comprehensive reference on Chinese Metaphysics, and an absolute must-have for all students, scholars, and practitioners of Chinese Metaphysics.

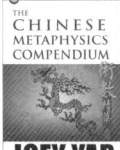

The Ten Thousand Year Calendar (Pocket Edition)

The Ten Thousand Year Calendar

Dong Gong Date Selection

The Date Selection Compendium

Plum Blossoms Divination Reference Book

San Yuan Dragon Gate Eight Formations Water Method

Xuan Kong Da Gua Ten Thousand Year Calendar

Bazi Hour Pillar Useful Gods - Wood

Bazi Hour Pillar Useful Gods - Fire

Bazi Hour Pillar Useful Gods - Earth

Bazi Hour Pillar Useful Gods - Metal

Bazi Hour Pillar Useful Gods - Water

Xuan Kong Da Gua Structures Reference Book

Xuan Kong Da Gua 64 Gua Transformation Analysis

Bazi Structures and Structural Useful Gods - Wood

Bazi Structures and Structural Useful Gods - Fire

Bazi Structures and Structural Useful Gods - Earth

Bazi Structures and Structural Useful Gods - Metal

Bazi Structures and Structural Useful Gods - Water

Xuan Kong Purple White Script

Earth Study Discern Truth Second Edition

www.masteryacademy.com | +603 - 2284 8080

Joey Yap's BaZi Profiling System

Three Levels of BaZi Profiling (English & Chinese versions)

In BaZi Profiling, there are three levels that reflect three different stages of a person's personal nature and character structure.

Level 1 – The Day Master

The Day Master in a nutshell is the BASIC YOU. The inborn personality. It is your essential character. It answers the basic question "WHO AM I". There are ten basic personality profiles – the TEN Day Masters – each with its unique set of personality traits, likes and dislikes.

Level 2 – The Structure

The Structure is your behavior and attitude – in other words, how you use your personality. It expands on the Day Master (Level 1). The structure reveals your natural tendencies in life – are you more controlling, more of a creator, supporter, thinker or connector? Each of the Ten Day Masters express themselves differently through the FIVE Structures. Why do we do the things we do? Why do we like the things we like? – The answers are in our BaZi STRUCTURE.

Level 3 – The Profile

The Profile reveals your unique abilities and skills, the masks that you consciously and unconsciously "put on" as you approach and navigate the world. Your Profile speaks of your ROLES in life. There are TEN roles – or Ten BaZi Profiles. Everyone plays a different role.

What makes you happy and what does success mean to you is different to somebody else. Your sense of achievement and sense of purpose in life is unique to your Profile. Your Profile will reveal your unique style.

The path of least resistance to your success and wealth can only be accessed once you get into your "flow." Your BaZi Profile reveals how you can get FLOW. It will show you your patterns in work, relationship and social settings. Being AWARE of these patterns is your first step to positive Life Transformation.

www.baziprofiling.com

BaZi Collections

Leading Chinese Astrology Master Trainer Joey Yap makes it easy to learn how to unlock your Destiny through your BaZi with these books. BaZi or Four Pillars of Destiny is an ancient Chinese science which enables individuals to understand their personality, hidden talents and abilities as well as their luck cycle, simply by examining the information contained within their birth data.

Understand and appreciate more about this astoundingly accurate ancient Chinese Metaphysical science with this BaZi Collection.

Feng Shui Collection

Must-Haves for Property Analysis!

For homeowners, those looking to build their own home or even investors who are looking to apply Feng Shui to their homes, these series of books provides valuable information from the classical Feng Shui therioes and applications.

In his trademark straight-to-the-point manner, Joey shares with you the Feng Shui do's and dont's when it comes to finding a property with favorable Feng Shui, which is condusive for home living.

Stories & Lessons on Feng Shui Series

All in all, this series is a delightful chronicle of Joey's articles, thoughts and vast experience - as a professional Feng Shui consultant and instructor - that have been purposely refined, edited and expanded upon to make for a light-hearted, interesting yet educational read. And with Feng Shui, BaZi, Mian Xiang and Yi Jing all thrown into this one dish, there's something for everyone.

www.masteryacademy.com | +603 - 2284 8080

Continue Your Journey with Joey Yap Books in Feng Shui

Pure Feng Shui
Pure Feng Shui is Joey Yap's debut with an international publisher, CICO Books, and is a refreshing and elegant look at the intricacies of Classical Feng Shui – now compiled in a useful manner for modern-day readers. This book is a comprehensive introduction to all the important precepts and techniques of Feng Shui practice.

Your Aquarium Here
This book is the first in Fengshuilogy Series, a series of matter-in-fact and useful Feng Shui books designed for the person who wants to do a fuss-free Feng Shui.

Xuan Kong Flying Stars
This book is an essential introductory book to the subject of Xuan Kong Fei Xing, a well-known and popular system of Feng Shui. Learn 'tricks of the trade' and 'trade secrets' to enhance and maximize Qi in your home or office.

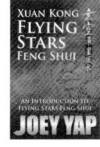

Walking the Dragons
Compiled in one book for the first time from Joey Yap's Feng Shui Mastery Excursion Series, the book highlights China's extensive, vibrant history with astute observations on the Feng Shui of important sites and places. Learn the landform formations of Yin Houses (tombs and burial places), as well as mountains, temples, castles, and villages.

The Art of Date Selection: Personal Date Selection
With the *Art of Date Selection: Personal Date Selection*, learn simple, practical methods you can employ to select not just good dates, but personalized good dates. Whether it's a personal activity such as a marriage or professional endeavor such as launching a business, signing a contract or even acquiring assets, this book will show you how to pick the good dates and tailor them to suit the activity in question, as well as avoid the negative ones too!

www.masteryacademy.com | +603 - 2284 8080

Face Reading Collection

Discover Face Reding (English & Chinese versions)

This is a comprehensive book on all areas of Face Reading, covering some of the most important facial features, including the forehead, mouth, ears and even philtrum above your lips. This book eill help you analyse not just your Destiny but help you achieve your full potential and achieve life fulfillment.

Joey Yap's Art of Face Reading

The Art of Face Reading is Joey Yap's second effort with CICO Books, and takes a lighter, more practical approach to Face Reading. This book does not so much focus on the individual features as it does on reading the entire face. It is about identifying common personality types and characters.

Easy Guide on Face Reading (English & Chinese versions)

The Face Reading Essentials series of books comprises 5 individual books on the key features of the face – Eyes, Eyebrows, Ears, Nose, and Mouth. Each book provides a detailed illustration and a simple yet descriptive explanation on the individual types of the features.

The books are equally useful and effective for beginners, enthusiasts, and the curious. The series is designed to enable people who are new to Face Reading to make the most of first impressions and learn to apply Face Reading skills to understand the personality and character of friends, family, co-workers, and even business associates.

Annual Releases
2011 Annual Outlook & Tong Shu

| Chinese Astrology for 2011 | Feng Shui for 2011 | Tong Shu Desktop Calendar 2011 | Professional Tong Shu Diary 2011 | Tong Shu Monthly Planner 2011 | Weekly Tong Shu Diary 2011 |

www.masteryacademy.com | +603 - 2284 8080

Educational Tools and Software

Xuan Kong Flying Stars Feng Shui Software
The Essential Application for Enthusiasts and Professionals

The Xuan Kong Flying Stars Feng Shui Software will assist you in the practice of Xuan Kong Feng Shui with minimum fuss and maximum effectiveness. Superimpose the Flying Stars charts over your house plans (or those of your clients) to clearly demarcate the 9 Palaces. Use it to help you create fast and sophisticated chart drawings and presentations, as well as to assist professional practitioners in the report-writing process before presenting the final reports for your clients. Students can use it to practice their Xuan Kong Feng Shui skills and knowledge, and it can even be used by designers and architects!

BaZi Ming Pan Software Version 2.0
Professional Four Pillars Calculator for Destiny Analysis

The BaZi Ming Pan Version 2.0 Professional Four Pillars Calculator for Destiny Analysis is the most technically advanced software of its kind in the world today. It allows even those without any knowledge of BaZi to generate their own BaZi Charts, and provides virtually every detail required to undertake a comprehensive Destiny Analysis.

This Professional Four Pillars Calculator allows you to even undertake a day-to-day analysis of your Destiny. What's more, all BaZi Charts generated by this software are fully printable and configurable! Designed for both enthusiasts and professional practitioners, this state-of-the-art software blends details with simplicity, and is capable of generating 4 different types of BaZi charts: **BaZi Professional Charts, BaZi Annual Analysis Charts, BaZi Pillar Analysis Charts and BaZi Family Relationship Charts.**

Joey Yap Feng Shui Template Set

Directions are the cornerstone of any successful Feng Shui audit or application. The **Joey Yap Feng Shui Template Set** is a set of three templates to simplify the process of taking directions and determining locations and positions, whether it's for a building, a house, or an open area such as a plot of land, all with just a floor plan or area map.

The Set comprises 3 basic templates: The Basic Feng Shui Template, 8 Mansions Feng Shui Template, and the Flying Stars Feng Shui Template.

Mini Feng Shui Compass

The Mini Feng Shui Compass is a self-aligning compass that is not only light at 100gms but also built sturdily to ensure it will be convenient to use anywhere. The rings on the Mini Feng Shui Compass are bi-lingual and incorporate the 24 Mountain Rings that is used in your traditional Luo Pan.

The comprehensive booklet included will guide you in applying the 24 Mountain Directions on your Mini Feng Shui Compass effectively and the 8 Mansions Feng Shui to locate the most auspicious locations within your home, office and surroundings. You can also use the Mini Feng Shui Compass when measuring the direction of your property for the purpose of applying Flying Stars Feng Shui.

www.masteryacademy.com | +603 - 2284 8080

Educational Tools and Software

Xuan Kong Vol.1
An Advanced Feng Shui Home Study Course

Learn the Xuan Kong Flying Star Feng Shui system in just 20 lessons! Joey Yap's specialised notes and course work have been written to enable distance learning without compromising on the breadth or quality of the syllabus. Learn at your own pace with the same material students in a live class would use. The most comprehensive distance learning course on Xuan Kong Flying Star Feng Shui in the market. Xuan Kong Flying Star Vol.1 comes complete with a special binder for all your course notes.

Feng Shui for Period 8 - (DVD)

Don't miss the Feng Shui Event of the next 20 years! Catch Joey Yap LIVE and find out just what Period 8 is all about. This DVD boxed set zips you through the fundamentals of Feng Shui and the impact of this important change in the Feng Shui calendar. Joey's entertaining, conversational style walks you through the key changes that Period 8 will bring and how to tap into Wealth Qi and Good Feng Shui for the next 20 years.

Xuan Kong Flying Stars Beginners Workshop - (DVD)

Take a front row seat in Joey Yap's Xuan Kong Flying Stars workshop with this unique LIVE RECORDING of Joey Yap's Xuan Kong Flying Stars Feng Shui workshop, attended by over 500 people. This DVD program provides an effective and quick introduction of Xuan Kong Feng Shui essentials for those who are just starting out in their study of classical Feng Shui. Learn to plot your own Flying Star chart in just 3 hours. Learn 'trade secret' methods, remedies and cures for Flying Stars Feng Shui. This boxed set contains 3 DVDs and 1 workbook with notes and charts for reference.

BaZi Four Pillars of Destiny Beginners Workshop - (DVD)

Ever wondered what Destiny has in store for you? Or curious to know how you can learn more about your personality and inner talents? BaZi or Four Pillars of Destiny is an ancient Chinese science that enables us to understand a person's hidden talent, inner potential, personality, health and wealth luck from just their birth data. This specially compiled DVD set of Joey Yap's BaZi Beginners Workshop provides a thorough and comprehensive introduction to BaZi. Learn how to read your own chart and understand your own luck cycle. This boxed set contains 3 DVDs and 1 workbook with notes and reference charts.

www.masteryacademy.com | +603 - 2284 8080

DVD Series

Joey Yap's Face Reading Revealed DVD Series

Mian Xiang, the Chinese art of Face Reading, is an ancient form of physiognomy and entails the use of the face and facial characteristics to evaluate key aspects of a person's life, luck and destiny. In his Face Reading DVDs series, Joey Yap shows you how the facial features reveal a wealth of information about a person's luck, destiny and personality.

Mian Xiang also tell us the talents, quirks and personality of an individual. Do you know that just by looking at a person's face, you can ascertain his or her health, wealth, relationships and career? Let Joey Yap show you how the 12 Palaces can be utilised to reveal a person's inner talents, characteristics and much more.

Feng Shui for Homebuyers DVD Series

In these DVDs, you will also learn how to identify properties with good Feng Shui features that will help you promote a fulfilling life and achieve your full potential. Discover how to avoid properties with negative Feng Shui that can bring about detrimental effects to your health, wealth and relationships.

Joey will also elaborate on how to fix the various aspects of your home that may have an impact on the Feng Shui of your property and give pointers on how to tap into the positive energies to support your goals.

Discover Feng Shui with Joey Yap: Set of 4 DVDs
Informative and entertaining, classical Feng Shui comes alive in *Discover Feng Shui with Joey Yap!*

You have the questions. Now let Joey personally answer them in this 4-set DVD compilation! Learn how to ensure the viability of your residence or workplace, Feng Shui-wise, without having to convert it into a Chinese antiques' shop. Classical Feng Shui is about harnessing the natural power of your environment to improve quality of life. It's a systematic and subtle metaphysical science.

Walking the Dragons with Joey Yap (The TV Series)

This DVD set features eight episodes, covering various landform Feng Shui analyses and applications from Joey Yap as he and his co-hosts travel through China. It includes case studies of both modern and historical sites with a focus on Yin House (burial places) Feng Shui and the tombs of the Qing Dynasty emperors.

The series was partly filmed on-location in mainland China, and the state of Selangor, Malaysia.

---

www.masteryacademy.com | +603 - 2284 8080

Home Study Courses

Gain Valuable Knowledge from the Comfort of Your Home

Now, armed with your trusty computer or laptop and Internet access, knowledge of Chinese Metaphysics is just a click away!

3 easy steps to activate your Home Study Course:

Step 1:
Go to the URL as indicated on the Activation Card, and key in your Activation Code

Step 2:
At the Registration page, fill in the details accordingly to enable us to generate your Student Identification (Student ID).

Step 3:
Upon successful registration, you may begin your lessons immediately.

Joey Yap's Feng Shui Mastery HomeStudy Course

Module 1: **Empowering Your Home**
Module 2: **Master Practitioner Program**

Learn how easy it is to harness the power of the environment to promote health, wealth and prosperity in your life. The knowledge and applications of Feng Shui will no more be a mystery but a valuable tool you can master on your own.

Joey Yap's BaZi Mastery HomeStudy Course

Module 1: **Mapping Your Life**
Module 2: **Mastering Your Future**

Discover your path of least resistance to success with insights about your personality and capabilities, and what strengths you can tap on to maximize your potential for success and happiness by mastering BaZi (Chinese Astrology). This course will teach you all the essentials you need to interpret a BaZi chart and more.

Joey Yap's Mian Xiang Mastery HomeStudy Course

Module 1: **Face Reading**
Module 2: **Advanced Face Reading**

A face can reveal so much about a person. Now, you can learn the art and science of Mian Xiang (Chinese Face Reading) to understand a person's character based on his or her facial features with ease and confidence.

www.masteryacademy.com | +603 - 2284 8080

Feng Shui Mastery™
LIVE COURSES (MODULES ONE TO FOUR)

The Feng Shui Mastery™ comprises Feng Shui Mastery Modules 1, 2, 3 and 4. It starts off with a foundation program up to the advanced practitioner level. It is a thorough, comprehensive program that covers important theories from various classical Feng Shui systems including Ba Zhai, San Yuan, San He, and Xuan Kong.

Module One:
Beginners Course

Module Two:
Practitioners Course

Module Three:
Advanced Practitioners Course

Module Four:
Master Course

BaZi Mastery™
LIVE COURSES (MODULES ONE TO FOUR)

The BaZi Mastery™ consists of BaZi Mastery Modules 1, 2, 3 and 4. In Modules 1 and 2, students will receive a thorough introduction to BaZi, along with an intensive understanding of BaZi principles and the requisite skills to practice it with accuracy and precision. This will prepare them, and serious Feng Shui practitioners, for a more advanced levels and fine-tune their application skills in Modules 3 and 4.

Module One:
Intensive Foundation Course

Module Two:
Practitioners Course

Module Three:
Advanced Practitioners Course

Module Four:
Master Course in BaZi

Xuan Kong Mastery™
LIVE COURSES (MODULES ONE TO THREE)
* Advanced Courses For Master Practitioners

The Xuan Kong Mastery™ comprises Xuan Kong Mastery Modules 1, 2A, 2B and 3. It is a sophisticated branch of Feng Shui replete with many techniques and formulae, enabling practitioners to evaluate Feng Shui on a more thorough and in-depth basis. The study of Xuan Kong encompasses numerology, symbology and science of the Ba Gua along with the mathematics of time.

Module One:
Advanced Foundation Course

Module Two A:
Advanced Xuan Kong Methodologies

Module Two B:
Purple White

Module Three:
Advanced Xuan Kong Da Gua

www.masteryacademy.com | +603 - 2284 8080

Mian Xiang Mastery™
LIVE COURSES (MODULES ONE AND TWO)

The Mian Xiang Mastery™ comprises of Mian Xiang Mastery Modules 1 and 2 to allow students to learn this ancient art in a thorough, detailed manner. Each module has a carefully-developed syllabus that allows students to get acquainted with the fundamentals of Mian Xiang before moving on to the more intricate theories and principles that will enable them to practice Mian Xiang with greater depth and complexity.

Module One:
Basic Face Reading

Module Two:
Practical Face Reading

Yi Jing Mastery™
LIVE COURSES (MODULES ONE AND TWO)

The Yi Jing Mastery™ comprises Modules 1 and 2. Both Modules aim to give casual and serious Yi Jing enthusiasts a serious insight into one of the most important philosophical treatises in ancient Chinese thought. Yi Jing uses sophisticated formulas and calculations to derive the answers to questions we pose. It is a science of divination, and in our classes there is a heavy emphasis on the scientific aspect of it. It bears no religious or superstitious affiliation.

Module One:
Traditional Yi Jing

Module Two:
Plum Blossom Numerology

Ze Ri Mastery™
LIVE COURSES (MODULES ONE AND TWO)

The ZeRi Mastery™ consists of ZeRi Mastery Modules 1 and 2. This program provides students with a thorough introduction to the art of Date Selection both for Personal and Feng Shui purposes. Our ZeRi Mastery™ aims to provide a thorough and comprehensive program on the art of Date Selection, covering everything from Personal and Feng Shui Date Selection to Xuan Kong Da Gua Date Selection.

Module One:
Personal and Feng Shui Date Selection

Module Two:
Xuan Kong Da Gua Date Selection

www.masteryacademy.com | +603 - 2284 8080

Feng Shui for Life

This is an entry-level five-day course designed for the Feng Shui beginner to learn the application of practical Feng Shui in day-to-day living. Lessons include quick tips on analyzing the BaZi chart, simple Feng Shui solutions for the home, basic Date Selection, useful Face Reading techniques and practical Water formulas. A great introduction course on Chinese Metaphysics studies for beginners.

Joey Yap's
Design Your Destiny

This is a three-day life transformation program designed to inspire awareness and action for you to create a better quality of life. It introduces the DRT™ (Decision Referential Technology) method, which utilizes the BaZi Personality Profiling system to determine the right version of you, and serves as a tool to help you make better decisions and achieve a better life in the least resistant way possible based on your Personality Profile Type.

Walk the Mountains! Learn Feng Shui in a Practical and Hands-on Program

 ## Feng Shui Mastery Excursion™

Learn landform (Luan Tou) Feng Shui by walking the mountains and chasing the Dragon's vein in China. This Program takes the students in a study tour to examine notable Feng Shui landmarks, mountains, hills, valleys, ancient palaces, famous mansions, houses and tombs in China. The Excursion is a 'practical' hands-on course where students are shown to perform readings using the formulas they've learnt and to recognize and read Feng Shui Landform (Luan Tou) formations.

Read about China Excursion here:
http://www.fengshuiexcursion.com

Mastery Academy courses are conducted around the world. Find out when will Joey Yap be in your area by visiting **www.masteryacademy.com** or call our office at **+603-2284 8080**.

---

www.masteryacademy.com | +603 - 2284 8080